JUMBLE®
CROSSWORDS™
Jackpot

A Treasure Trove of Puzzling Fun

David L. Hoyt

TRIUMPH
BOOKS

CHICAGO

This book is available in quantity at special discounts
for your group or organization.
For further information, contact:

Triumph Books
601 South LaSalle Street
Suite 500
Chicago, Illinois 60605
(312) 939-3330
Fax (312) 663-3557

Printed in the United States of America

ISBN 9781572436152

Contents

JUMBLE® CROSSWORDS™
Jackpot

PUZZLE #1

JUMBLE CROSSWORDS™

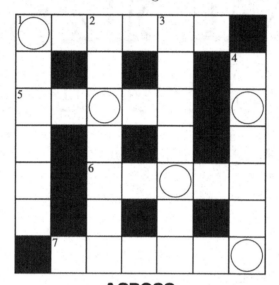

ACROSS

CLUE	ANSWER
1. _____ Harbor	N B O O T S
5. _____ tortoise	A N I T G
6. Home to the Île de la Cité	R P I A S
7. South American city	G A O O T B

DOWN

CLUE	ANSWER
1. Important person	W G I G I B
2. Cleanser	H O P M O S A
3. Second largest of its kind	T I R A O O N
4. Largest of its kind	A R I S S U

CLUE: This island is about 19 miles by 4 miles.

BONUS ◯◯◯◯◯

How to play — Complete the crossword puzzle by looking at the clues and unscrambling the answers. When the puzzle is complete, unscramble the circled letters to solve the bonus.

JUMBLE CROSSWORDS™

ACROSS

CLUE	ANSWER
1. Flag	N B A E R N
5. Right	X C T E A
6. Expression	M I O I D
7. Exit	R G S S E E

DOWN

CLUE	ANSWER
1. Whiten	E L B H A C
2. Approaching	A E N I R G N
3. Entangle	W I T N N E E
4. Universe	M S O O C S

CLUE: The first sport to be filmed (1894).

BONUS

How to play   Complete the crossword puzzle by looking at the clues and unscrambling the answers. When the puzzle is complete, unscramble the circled letters to solve the bonus.

JUMBLE CROSSWORDS™

ACROSS

CLUE	ANSWER
1. Reason	E M V O I T
5. Subject	T E E H M
6. Detects	N I F S D
7. English river	H A T S E M

DOWN

CLUE	ANSWER
1. Slow _____	T M N I O O
2. Like December	E T L T F W H
3. Asian country	N T E I M A V
4. Cooks	A O R T S S

CLUE: This U.S. city got its name from the French word meaning "the narrow place."

BONUS

How to play Complete the crossword puzzle by looking at the clues and unscrambling the answers. When the puzzle is complete, unscramble the circled letters to solve the bonus.

JUMBLE CROSSWORDS™

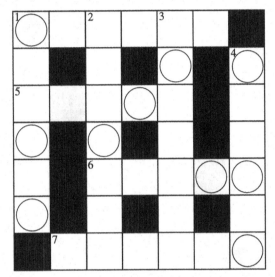

ACROSS

CLUE	ANSWER
1. Counter	A A S U C B
5. Reward	R E Z I P
6. Tossed	H T W E R
7. Sea _____	N R H I C U

DOWN

CLUE	ANSWER
1. Drawing power	P E P L A A
2. Pilot	R V O A T I A
3. Find	N E U R A H T
4. Australian city	D A N I W R

BONUS CLUE: Home to Mount Cook (highest point).

How to play — Complete the crossword puzzle by looking at the clues and unscrambling the answers. When the puzzle is complete, unscramble the circled letters to solve the bonus.

PUZZLE #5

JUMBLE CROSSWORDS™

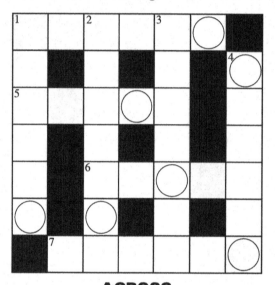

ACROSS

CLUE	ANSWER
1. Shoddy	B H Y B S A
5. Furious	A I B D R
6. Changes	S E T D I
7. Says	R T E T S U

DOWN

CLUE	ANSWER
1. Able-bodied	R T O G N S
2. Encompassing	T A N M E I B
3. _____ story	M E E B I D T
4. Searches	K R S I F S

CLUE: Mean

BONUS

How to play · Complete the crossword puzzle by looking at the clues and unscrambling the answers. When the puzzle is complete, unscramble the circled letters to solve the bonus.

JUMBLE CROSSWORDS™

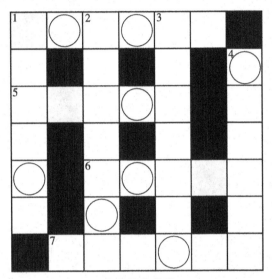

ACROSS

CLUE	ANSWER
1. _____-bound	L C S U E M
5. Small fish	T S L E M
6. Discredit	A N I T T
7. 1984 movie	M C A I E N

DOWN

CLUE	ANSWER
1. Symbolic figure	A S M T O C
2. Cynic	E C I K S T P
3. Alkali metal	M I U H I L T
4. Defeated	T A B N E E

CLUE: A large river or a state capital.

BONUS

How to play Complete the crossword puzzle by looking at the clues and unscrambling the answers. When the puzzle is complete, unscramble the circled letters to solve the bonus.

#7

JUMBLE CROSSWORDS™

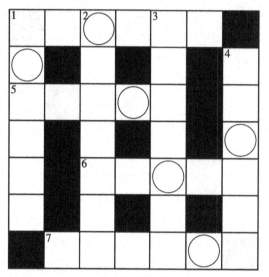

ACROSS

CLUE	ANSWER
1. Foolish	N S W E I U
5. Tooth	R M A O L
6. Repeatedly	F E T N O
7. Deadly	H T E A L L

DOWN

CLUE	ANSWER
1. Reveal	M N K S A U
2. Pleasing	E E M W O C L
3. Scribble	R C S T H C A
4. _____ column	L A N S I P

CLUE: Home to the Chungyang mountain range.

BONUS

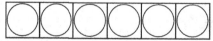

How to play Complete the crossword puzzle by looking at the clues and unscrambling the answers. When the puzzle is complete, unscramble the circled letters to solve the bonus.

JUMBLE CROSSWORDS™

ACROSS

CLUE	ANSWER
1. Magnetism	ULRLEA
5. Contributes	EVSIG
6. Blow up	TUSBR
7. European city	NEGAEV

DOWN

CLUE	ANSWER
1. African country	NGALAO
2. Enchanting	LLEOBAV
3. Hold	EESRREV
4. G.W.'s wife	RAMHAT

CLUE: Flag=

WHITE
GREEN
RED

BONUS ◯◯◯◯◯◯◯◯

How to play Complete the crossword puzzle by looking at the clues and unscrambling the answers. When the puzzle is complete, unscramble the circled letters to solve the bonus.

PUZZLE #9

JUMBLE® CROSSWORDS™

ACROSS

CLUE	ANSWER
1. Foreign _____	LYOPIC
5. Weasel family member	BSAEL
6. Increase	AEISR
7. Dormant	TNETAL

DOWN

CLUE	ANSWER
1. Pale color	ASPLET
2. Home to Monrovia	BILREIA
3. Narrow opening	ERCIVEC
4. Unpretentious	DOMETS

CLUE: A federation consisting of 13 states.

BONUS

How to play   Complete the crossword puzzle by looking at the clues and unscrambling the answers. When the puzzle is complete, unscramble the circled letters to solve the bonus.

10

JUMBLE CROSSWORDS™

ACROSS

CLUE	ANSWER
1. Thing, individual	TNIYET
5. Lively	YEPPP
6. Creature of folklore	LTORL
7. Restraint	DIRELB

DOWN

CLUE	ANSWER
1. Anticipate	XPTEEC
2. Informant	PITTSRE
3. _____ gland	HIYORTD
4. (1 + 2) x 3 + 3	LEWTEV

CLUE: Animal

BONUS

How to play   Complete the crossword puzzle by looking at the clues and unscrambling the answers. When the puzzle is complete, unscramble the circled letters to solve the bonus.

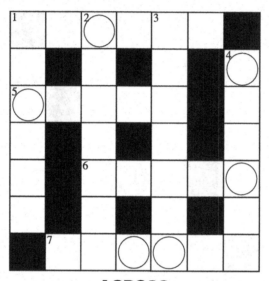

JUMBLE CROSSWORDS™

ACROSS

CLUE	ANSWER
1. Harsh	NNIKDU
5. Fashion	TLEYS
6. "Crude" workman	LERIO
7. Stopped	AECDES

DOWN

CLUE	ANSWER
1. Not acknowledged	NNUUGS
2. _____ address	YNEKOET
3. Torments	EEESLND
4. Shocking	ROHIRD

CLUE: There are about 370 species of these.

BONUS

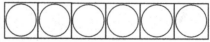

How to play Complete the crossword puzzle by looking at the clues and unscrambling the answers. When the puzzle is complete, unscramble the circled letters to solve the bonus.

JUMBLE® CROSSWORDS™

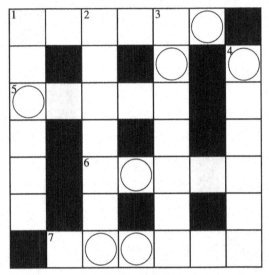

ACROSS

CLUE		ANSWER
1.	Slick	LSYGOS
5.	_____ point	RTXAE
6.	Mass of metal	NOIGT
7.	Sell	LDDEEP

DOWN

CLUE		ANSWER
1.	Elbow _____	RGSAEE
2.	Summary	LITNUEO
3.	Caught	NGSGDEA
4.	Type of vessel	TEELTK

CLUE: The first U.S. president who was born in the 20th century.

BONUS

How to play Complete the crossword puzzle by looking at the clues and unscrambling the answers. When the puzzle is complete, unscramble the circled letters to solve the bonus.

13

#13

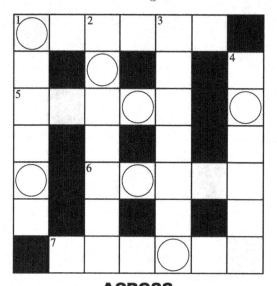

JUMBLE® CROSSWORDS™

ACROSS

CLUE	ANSWER
1. Close	R N A E Y B
5. _____ Bay	A A P T M
6. Bring about	N T C A E
7. On land	H S A E R O

DOWN

CLUE	ANSWER
1. Fool	T I N I W T
2. Random	M S I E L S A
3. Swaggering conduct	R V D A A B O
4. Hate	A O L E H T

CLUE: You must *have* one to *give* one.

BONUS ◯◯◯◯◯◯◯

How to play — Complete the crossword puzzle by looking at the clues and unscrambling the answers. When the puzzle is complete, unscramble the circled letters to solve the bonus.

#14

JUMBLE CROSSWORDS™

ACROSS

CLUE	ANSWER
1. Type of muscles	B S P I E C
5. Small club	A O T N B
6. Extraneous	L E I N A
7. Practical	E U U S L F

DOWN

CLUE	ANSWER
1. Variety of lynx	T O A B C B
2. Curving weapon	A T U L S S C
3. Religious figure	F N O P I T F
4. Indication	A I N G L S

CLUE: Legendary place

BONUS

How to play Complete the crossword puzzle by looking at the clues and unscrambling the answers. When the puzzle is complete, unscramble the circled letters to solve the bonus.

JUMBLE CROSSWORDS™

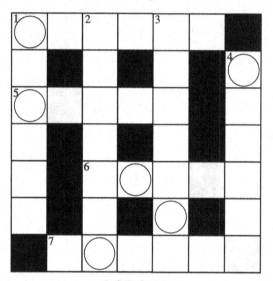

ACROSS

CLUE	ANSWER
1. Wonder	A L E M V R
5. Headband	R I A A T
6. Hamilton _____	L I N T E
7. _____ road	E R D E F E

DOWN

CLUE	ANSWER
1. Joint	T A M L U U
2. Achieve	A E R I L E Z
3. Empowered	D E L E N B A
4. Swivelling wheel	R A S C E T

CLUE: David O. Saylor patented a type of this in 1871.

BONUS ○○○○○○

How to play — Complete the crossword puzzle by looking at the clues and unscrambling the answers. When the puzzle is complete, unscramble the circled letters to solve the bonus.

#16

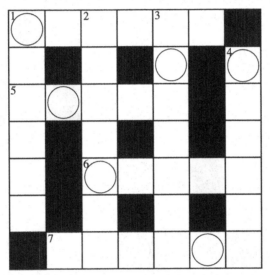

JUMBLE® CROSSWORDS™

ACROSS

CLUE		ANSWER
1.	_____ River	GITIRS
5.	Period of time	NTTIS
6.	Strong feeling	RNEAG
7.	Scourge	REOTRR

DOWN

CLUE		ANSWER
1.	Tried	TSEDET
2.	Facial expression	AMICRGE
3.	1, for example	NRIEETG
4.	Not as wealthy	RPREOO

CLUE: 1970 "Best Picture"

BONUS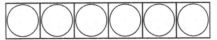

How to play   Complete the crossword puzzle by looking at the clues and unscrambling the answers. When the puzzle is complete, unscramble the circled letters to solve the bonus.

JUMBLE CROSSWORDS™

ACROSS

CLUE	ANSWER
1. See	BLEDOH
5. Discompose	PETSU
6. Creamy mixture	NICIG
7. Grouped together	MTADEE

DOWN

CLUE	ANSWER
1. Contusion	URBIES
2. Unfriendly	THSOIEL
3. _____ fluoride	MLUIHIT
4. Counterfeited	ROGFDE

CLUE: One variety of this can survive out of water for more than a day.

BONUS

How to play — Complete the crossword puzzle by looking at the clues and unscrambling the answers. When the puzzle is complete, unscramble the circled letters to solve the bonus.

#18

JUMBLE CROSSWORDS™

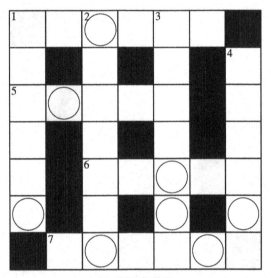

ACROSS

CLUE	ANSWER
1. Home to Papeete	HITTAI
5. Home style	DUOTR
6. Mythical hunter	RNIOO
7. Climb	NSTAEC

DOWN

CLUE	ANSWER
1. Teachers	UTOTSR
2. Offensive	DIHOESU
3. Steam _____	BRIUTEN
4. Attractive body	AETMGN

CLUE: Light

BONUS

How to play — Complete the crossword puzzle by looking at the clues and unscrambling the answers. When the puzzle is complete, unscramble the circled letters to solve the bonus.

PUZZLE #19

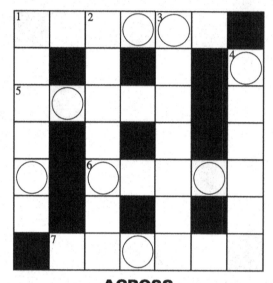

JUMBLE CROSSWORDS™

ACROSS

CLUE	ANSWER
1. Expressions	MDIOIS
5. Type of aperture	LPIPU
6. _____ bar	NKCAS
7. Fought	UDDEEF

DOWN

CLUE	ANSWER
1. Urges	LESIPM
2. Predicament	PMISAES
3. Duck	LAAMLDR
4. Refused to proceed	KLEADB

CLUE: This U.S. state capital was named after a man who lived 500 years ago.

BONUS

How to play Complete the crossword puzzle by looking at the clues and unscrambling the answers. When the puzzle is complete, unscramble the circled letters to solve the bonus.

#20

JUMBLE CROSSWORDS™

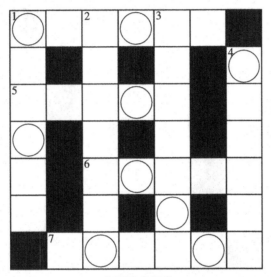

ACROSS

CLUE	ANSWER
1. Tattered	BAHSYB
5. Stick	LNGIC
6. Arrangement	DRORE
7. Frank	NIACDD

DOWN

CLUE	ANSWER
1. Curved cutter	LICESK
2. One of 50	RAOZAIN
3. City on the Tigris	DDGBAAH
4. Dreaded	ARFDEE

CLUE: U.S. city on the Tanana River, home to 30,000.

BONUS

How to play — Complete the crossword puzzle by looking at the clues and unscrambling the answers. When the puzzle is complete, unscramble the circled letters to solve the bonus.

JUMBLE CROSSWORDS™

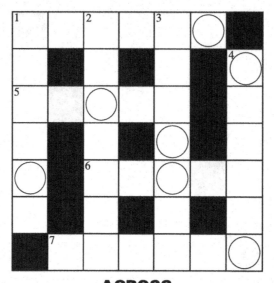

ACROSS

CLUE	ANSWER
1. Sound	RTSYUD
5. Accumulate	AASMS
6. Pipe _____	MRAED
7. Copy _____	DOREIT

DOWN

CLUE	ANSWER
1. Steady	AETSLB
2. Without help	NUIDDEA
3. Analyze	TDCISES
4. Hotter	RRMAEW

CLUE: Professional arguers

BONUS

How to play   Complete the crossword puzzle by looking at the clues and unscrambling the answers. When the puzzle is complete, unscramble the circled letters to solve the bonus.

#22

JUMBLE CROSSWORDS™

ACROSS

CLUE	ANSWER
1. Restore	EEVIRV
5. Nocturnal mammal	MLEUR
6. Symbols	LIOSD
7. Green _____	REBSTE

DOWN

CLUE	ANSWER
1. _____ map	LERFIE
2. Bloodsucker	MAEIVPR
3. Wordy	BREESOV
4. Sounds	NSISOE

CLUE: This TV host served in the U.S. Peace Corps in Panama from 1969-1970.

BONUS

How to play — Complete the crossword puzzle by looking at the clues and unscrambling the answers. When the puzzle is complete, unscramble the circled letters to solve the bonus.

PUZZLE

#23

JUMBLE CROSSWORDS™

ACROSS

CLUE	ANSWER
1. _____ Indian	HPCAEA
5. Large	TEYHF
6. Verge	NIRKB
7. Show	AEEVLR

DOWN

CLUE	ANSWER
1. European city	HTASNE
2. Gracious	BFAAELF
3. Crazy	YEAHIWR
4. Metal element	NLIEKC

CLUE: More than half the Earth's animal groups are found here.

BONUS ◯◯ ◯◯◯ ◯◯◯

How to play Complete the crossword puzzle by looking at the clues and unscrambling the answers. When the puzzle is complete, unscramble the circled letters to solve the bonus.

#24

JUMBLE CROSSWORDS™

ACROSS

CLUE		ANSWER
1.	Dumbfound	L B G E G O
5.	Pipe _____	M R D A E
6.	Type of seed	N A R O C
7.	Table _____	E I T N S N

DOWN

CLUE		ANSWER
1.	Confusion	D E L B M A
2.	Explosive device	E E R A N D G
3.	Ridicule	M A L O P N O
4.	Beverages	R I D S K N

CLUE: This U.S. president was born on the Fourth of July.

BONUS

How to play   Complete the crossword puzzle by looking at the clues and unscrambling the answers. When the puzzle is complete, unscramble the circled letters to solve the bonus.

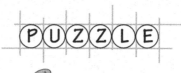

#25

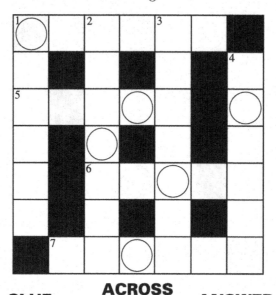

ACROSS

CLUE	ANSWER
1. Harsh ruler	TRYTAN
5. Brim	RSIOV
6. Rouse	KVOEE
7. Bets	ETKASS

DOWN

CLUE	ANSWER
1. Bar	AREVNT
2. Self-_____	ECEPSTR
3. Virginia city	RKONOFL
4. Emphasize	TSSSER

CLUE: The first vegetable grown in outer space.

BONUS

How to play   Complete the crossword puzzle by looking at the clues and unscrambling the answers. When the puzzle is complete, unscramble the circled letters to solve the bonus.

#26

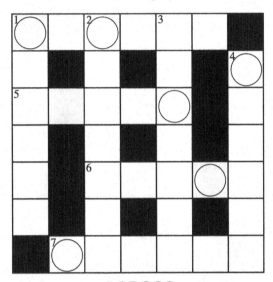

JUMBLE CROSSWORDS™

ACROSS

CLUE	ANSWER
1. Mean	NNIKDU
5. Aquatic carnivore	TORET
6. Liquor	HHCOO
7. Said	PNOESK

DOWN

CLUE	ANSWER
1. Ideal place	TUOIAP
2. Popular additive	EKPCTUH
3. _____ terrier	RFONOKL
4. Sea _____	NUIRHC

CLUE: Commotion

BONUS

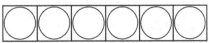

How to play   Complete the crossword puzzle by looking at the clues and unscrambling the answers. When the puzzle is complete, unscramble the circled letters to solve the bonus.

JUMBLE CROSSWORDS™

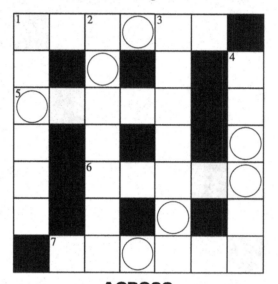

ACROSS

CLUE	ANSWER
1. Repeated	E O H D E C
5. Victor's opposition	R O E S L
6. Change	T A A P D
7. Badger	E C H E L K

DOWN

CLUE	ANSWER
1. Sign up	L N E I T S
2. _____ situation	E S O T G A H
3. Designate	A K E A M R R
4. Planet part	N A M E L T

CLUE: If you don't *take* this, you might *lose* it.

BONUS

How to play — Complete the crossword puzzle by looking at the clues and unscrambling the answers. When the puzzle is complete, unscramble the circled letters to solve the bonus.

#28

JUMBLE® CROSSWORDS™

ACROSS

CLUE	ANSWER
1. Call	N S O U M M
5. Recover	L A R Y L
6. Asian currency	E U P E R
7. Package	R C A L E P

DOWN

CLUE	ANSWER
1. Strange	R S W E Y C
2. Jungle disease	L A M I R A A
3. _____ Games	M O Y C I P L
4. Unveil	E R E A V L

CLUE: This former part of the U.S.S.R. is home to more than 3 million people.

BONUS

How to play   Complete the crossword puzzle by looking at the clues and unscrambling the answers. When the puzzle is complete, unscramble the circled letters to solve the bonus.

 #29

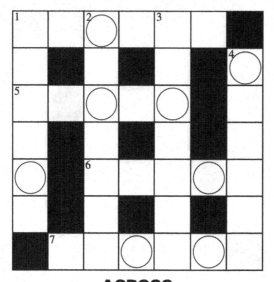

JUMBLE® CROSSWORDS™

ACROSS

CLUE	ANSWER
1. _____ oil	TCOSRA
5. Warrant	RIEMT
6. Knotted loop	EONSO
7. Astute	WHERDS

DOWN

CLUE	ANSWER
1. Fighting	MCTBOA
2. Crumple	RCSNUHC
3. Result	UCEOOTM
4. Rise	NSECAD

CLUE: Some of the desert scenes in this movie were filmed in Africa.

BONUS ⊙⊙⊙⊙ ⊙⊙⊙⊙

How to play Complete the crossword puzzle by looking at the clues and unscrambling the answers. When the puzzle is complete, unscramble the circled letters to solve the bonus.

JUMBLE® CROSSWORDS™

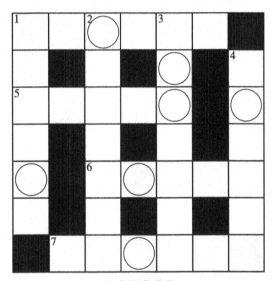

ACROSS

CLUE	ANSWER
1. Atomic _____	R M N E U B
5. Guiding principle	D E R C E
6. _____ song	H R C O T
7. European city	N O O D N L

DOWN

CLUE	ANSWER
1. Sweet liquid	E A R N T C
2. Master	A R O M T S E
3. Survived	R U D D E E N
4. _____ Hale	T A N N A H

CLUE: This performer's birth name is _____ Louise Veronica Ciccone.

BONUS

How to play Complete the crossword puzzle by looking at the clues and unscrambling the answers. When the puzzle is complete, unscramble the circled letters to solve the bonus.

JUMBLE CROSSWORDS™

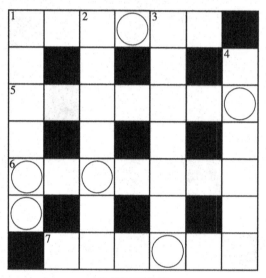

ACROSS

CLUE	ANSWER
1. Fleshy root	D A R S I H
5. Praise	L P A A P D U
6. Storm _____	R O T P O R E
7. Fixed	N E M D D E

DOWN

CLUE	ANSWER
1. Buildings and land	L A R E Y T
2. Bemoan	P E D O L E R
3. Busy	A S P M D E W
4. Cherished	D E R A D O

CLUE: Rarity

BONUS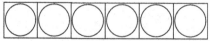

How to play
Complete the crossword puzzle by looking at the clues and unscrambling the answers. When the puzzle is complete, unscramble the circled letters to solve the bonus.

PUZZLE #32

JUMBLE CROSSWORDS™

ACROSS

CLUE		ANSWER
1.	Colleague	TORHOC
5.	Businesses	FSMIR
6.	_____ Island	LISEL
7.	Accumulates	ROTSES

DOWN

CLUE		ANSWER
1.	Treasury	FCREFO
2.	Pick	RAEVSHT
3.	Type of thief	TSLURRE
4.	Entertains	UAMESS

CLUE: Programs

BONUS

How to play — Complete the crossword puzzle by looking at the clues and unscrambling the answers. When the puzzle is complete, unscramble the circled letters to solve the bonus.

#33

JUMBLE® CROSSWORDS™

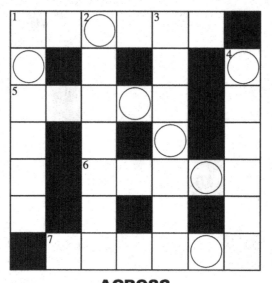

ACROSS

CLUE		ANSWER
1.	Instant	T M E M N O
5.	Break open	B R T U S
6.	Curve	R K O C O
7.	Thin-walled vessel	K A R B E E

DOWN

CLUE		ANSWER
1.	Packed	B O M D E B
2.	Wonder	R L I M C A E
3.	System	T E N O W K R
4.	Heart	K I T C E R

CLUE: "Abbott and Costello," for instance.

BONUS ◯◯◯◯◯◯◯

How to play   Complete the crossword puzzle by looking at the clues and unscrambling the answers. When the puzzle is complete, unscramble the circled letters to solve the bonus.

#34

JUMBLE CROSSWORDS™

ACROSS

CLUE	ANSWER
1. _____ enemy	M R O T L A
5. Bermuda, for example	R S A G S
6. Invigorating concoction	N I O T C
7. Hauls	K R C U S T

DOWN

CLUE	ANSWER
1. Strong	T Y I H M G
2. Agent	A E R T L R O
3. Atomic element "As"	R I A S N E C
4. Automotive components	K H O S S C

CLUE: You, for example.

BONUS

How to play — Complete the crossword puzzle by looking at the clues and unscrambling the answers. When the puzzle is complete, unscramble the circled letters to solve the bonus.

#35

JUMBLE CROSSWORDS™

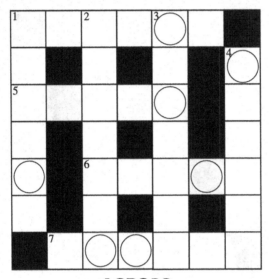

ACROSS

CLUE	ANSWER
1. Distinct article	ELCASU
5. Molten material	AAGMM
6. Stately	LERAG
7. Touched down	NALEDD

DOWN

CLUE	ANSWER
1. Rubber _____	MECTNE
2. Neighbor to Mauritania	LIGREAA
3. Caught	ADGENSG
4. Cried	WLDEAB

CLUE: Americans eat more than 11 billion of these each year.

BONUS ○○○○○○○

How to play — Complete the crossword puzzle by looking at the clues and unscrambling the answers. When the puzzle is complete, unscramble the circled letters to solve the bonus.

#36

JUMBLE CROSSWORDS™

ACROSS

CLUE	ANSWER
1. Wet	EAKDSO
5. Understand	AGRPS
6. Warm, dry room	UANAS
7. Arrival	TADEVN

DOWN

CLUE	ANSWER
1. Sign	LSAING
2. Gathered	AADESSM
3. Support	PSEUOES
4. Whole	NITCAT

BONUS

CLUE: $32°F = 0°C$

How to play   Complete the crossword puzzle by looking at the clues and unscrambling the answers. When the puzzle is complete, unscramble the circled letters to solve the bonus.

#37

JUMBLE CROSSWORDS™

ACROSS

CLUE	ANSWER
1. Home to Kampala	A G N U A D
5. Chocolate-brown color	M H C A O
6. Advice	P I T U N
7. More wicked	E E R M N A

DOWN

CLUE	ANSWER
1. Maximum	M U T S O T
2. Adduce	B S E A I C R
3. Blank	A E D D N A P
4. _____ cracker	R Y E O T S

CLUE: Alfred Nobel patented this in 1867.

BONUS

How to play — Complete the crossword puzzle by looking at the clues and unscrambling the answers. When the puzzle is complete, unscramble the circled letters to solve the bonus.

PUZZLE #38

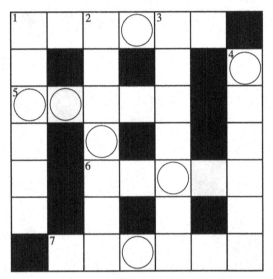

JUMBLE CROSSWORDS™

ACROSS

CLUE	ANSWER
1. Tense	ANSEYU
5. Failure	EORLS
6. Fibbing	NYIGL
7. Display	LUINEV

DOWN

CLUE	ANSWER
1. Different	LNEIKU
2. The fifth of its kind	PSELINO
3. Suppose	MRIUSSE
4. Region in India	NEBLAG

CLUE: This country borders five countries.

BONUS

How to play — Complete the crossword puzzle by looking at the clues and unscrambling the answers. When the puzzle is complete, unscramble the circled letters to solve the bonus.

PUZZLE #39

JUMBLE CROSSWORDS™

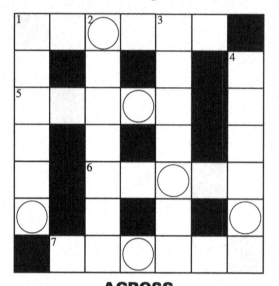

ACROSS

CLUE	ANSWER
1. _____ television	BIPUCL
5. Registered _____	RNSEU
6. _____ and _____	NIGAA
7. Giant _____	DNAASP

DOWN

CLUE	ANSWER
1. _____ pusher	NLIEPC
2. _____ Eden	RABBAAR
3. Northern _____	LEARNID
4. Soft _____	KRNISD

CLUE: _____ _____

BONUS ○○○○○○

How to play — Complete the crossword puzzle by looking at the clues and unscrambling the answers. When the puzzle is complete, unscramble the circled letters to solve the bonus.

#40

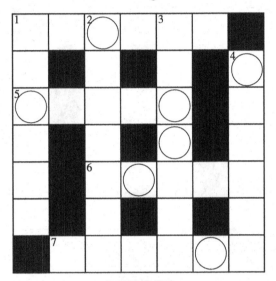

JUMBLE CROSSWORDS™

ACROSS

CLUE	ANSWER
1. Harm	M E D G A A
5. Coffee shop	N R E I D
6. Rough game	B R G Y U
7. Picked	H N E O S C

DOWN

CLUE	ANSWER
1. Eluded	D D D E O G
2. Ruler	H N O M R A C
3. Shelters	R A A G G S E
4. Paul _____	Y N U B A N

CLUE: Private automobiles were not allowed in this country until 1948.

BONUS

How to play   Complete the crossword puzzle by looking at the clues and unscrambling the answers. When the puzzle is complete, unscramble the circled letters to solve the bonus.

PUZZLE

#41

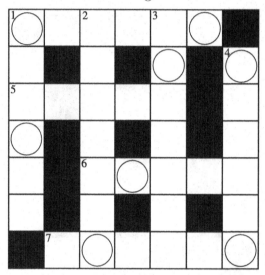

JUMBLE CROSSWORDS™

ACROSS

CLUE	ANSWER
1. _____ date	BDUOEL
5. Overturn	PTESU
6. Fourth of its kind	RLIPA
7. ATM's "T"	LETREL

DOWN

CLUE	ANSWER
1. Twos	UEDSEC
2. Draw attention away from	EPGATSU
3. Actual	TILRELA
4. Shout	LORELH

CLUE: Solve

BONUS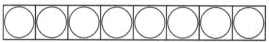

How to play — Complete the crossword puzzle by looking at the clues and unscrambling the answers. When the puzzle is complete, unscramble the circled letters to solve the bonus.

#42

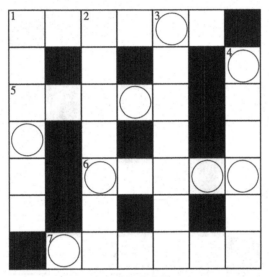

JUMBLE CROSSWORDS™

ACROSS

CLUE	ANSWER
1. Luminous	LCUETN
5. Step	TRIAS
6. Representations	DISLO
7. Chain _____	KMOSRE

DOWN

CLUE	ANSWER
1. European city	NLOBIS
2. Braincase	RACINMU
3. U.S. East Coast city	LRONKOF
4. Powerful spring	EERGSY

CLUE: "I don't have any . . . You may or may not."
D.L.H.

BONUS

How to play — Complete the crossword puzzle by looking at the clues and unscrambling the answers. When the puzzle is complete, unscramble the circled letters to solve the bonus.

PUZZLE #43

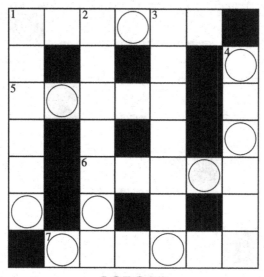

JUMBLE CROSSWORDS™

ACROSS

CLUE	ANSWER
1. Blocked	E A D D M M
5. Police _____	A G B E D
6. _____ up	L E C N A
7. Planned	T A L S D E

DOWN

CLUE	ANSWER
1. A large city	B U D N I L
2. _____ student	D M C L I A E
3. Chlorine is one	T E N E E M L
4. Shot	R U I D E N

CLUE: Good _____

BONUS ○○○○○○○○○

How to play   Complete the crossword puzzle by looking at the clues and unscrambling the answers. When the puzzle is complete, unscramble the circled letters to solve the bonus.

#44

JUMBLE CROSSWORDS™

ACROSS

CLUE	ANSWER
1. Couch _____	TPAOOT
5. Bush	RHSBU
6. _____ tower	YRVIO
7. Fought	UDDEFE

DOWN

CLUE	ANSWER
1. Water _____	LPOITS
2. Small destroyer	REETIMT
3. Newspaper	BOAITDL
4. Lifted	UYODBE

CLUE: This entertainer was born in London.

BONUS

How to play — Complete the crossword puzzle by looking at the clues and unscrambling the answers. When the puzzle is complete, unscramble the circled letters to solve the bonus.

PUZZLE #45

JUMBLE CROSSWORDS™

ACROSS

CLUE		ANSWER
1.	Misfortune	HMSIPA
5.	Type of musical instrument	ALIVO
6.	Phascolarctos cinereus	LOKAA
7.	"+"	ROTPNO

DOWN

CLUE		ANSWER
1.	Touching	NIMVOG
2.	Thriller	RHOSKEC
3.	Rigid	TANMAAD
4.	Keep	AEITNR

CLUE: Home to Gonder, Nazrét, and Diré Dawa.

BONUS

How to play — Complete the crossword puzzle by looking at the clues and unscrambling the answers. When the puzzle is complete, unscramble the circled letters to solve the bonus.

#46

JUMBLE CROSSWORDS™

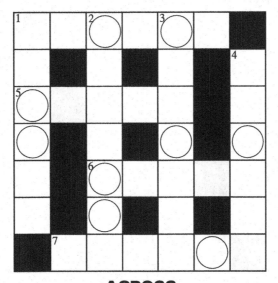

ACROSS

CLUE	ANSWER
1. Laugh	E K A C C L
5. Ninth of its kind	U L O T P
6. Mad	R I E A T
7. Type of pitch	L D I R S E

DOWN

CLUE	ANSWER
1. _____ Age	P O R P C E
2. Dire	U R A I C L C
3. Snow _____	R O E D A P L
4. Profession	E A R C R E

BONUS **CLUE:** Johan Vaaler invented this in 1899.

How to play — Complete the crossword puzzle by looking at the clues and unscrambling the answers. When the puzzle is complete, unscramble the circled letters to solve the bonus.

PUZZLE #47

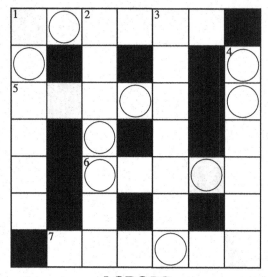

JUMBLE CROSSWORDS™

ACROSS

CLUE	ANSWER
1. A.J.'s bill	NEWYTT
5. Type of poplar	ANESP
6. Units of area	RCASE
7. Corners	ENSALG

DOWN

CLUE	ANSWER
1. English river	AHTSEM
2. Spell out	PEALIXN
3. Climbing plant part	LIRTNED
4. Shatters	RSBTSU

BONUS   **CLUE:** The largest of its kind.

◯◯◯◯   ◯◯◯◯◯◯

How to play   Complete the crossword puzzle by looking at the clues and unscrambling the answers. When the puzzle is complete, unscramble the circled letters to solve the bonus.

JUMBLE CROSSWORDS™

ACROSS

CLUE	ANSWER
1. Sprightly	BMNEIL
5. Soft palate	LMEUV
6. Classified	ARTDE
7. Delay	LADEDW

DOWN

CLUE	ANSWER
1. Greenhorn	ENCOIV
2. Type of disease	AIAMRAL
3. Restricted	MILTIDE
4. Walk laboriously	DURTEG

CLUE: Decision

BONUS

How to play — Complete the crossword puzzle by looking at the clues and unscrambling the answers. When the puzzle is complete, unscramble the circled letters to solve the bonus.

PUZZLE #49

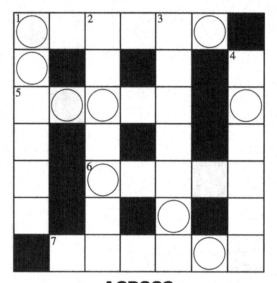

JUMBLE CROSSWORDS™

ACROSS

CLUE	ANSWER
1. Pilfered	P S I W D E
5. Objectionable	L W U F A
6. Urge	P M I L E
7. Controls	R T S S E E

DOWN

CLUE	ANSWER
1. Dilapidated	B A H Y S B
2. Impose	F N L I T I C
3. Surpass	E S L I C E P
4. Planets	R O D L S W

CLUE: _____ can swim at speeds faster than 50 mph.

BONUS ◯◯◯◯◯◯◯◯◯

How to play   Complete the crossword puzzle by looking at the clues and unscrambling the answers. When the puzzle is complete, unscramble the circled letters to solve the bonus.

#50

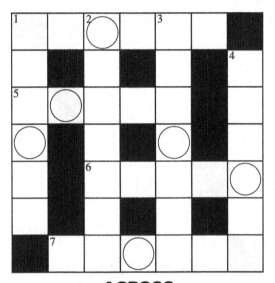

JUMBLE CROSSWORDS™

ACROSS

CLUE	ANSWER
1. Device	TDAEGG
5. Small amount of color	NGITE
6. Once more	AIANG
7. Blades	KTSSEA

DOWN

CLUE	ANSWER
1. Collect	TAGREH
2. Home to Frederiksberg	NEDAMKR
3. High class	LTNEAEG
4. Father of the Titans	AUNRSU

CLUE: 1982 "Best Picture"

BONUS

How to play — Complete the crossword puzzle by looking at the clues and unscrambling the answers. When the puzzle is complete, unscramble the circled letters to solve the bonus.

PUZZLE #51

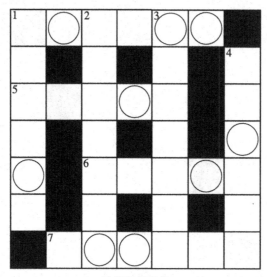

JUMBLE CROSSWORDS™

ACROSS

CLUE	ANSWER
1. Quick	MPORTP
5. Fashion	TLEYS
6. Box _____	ALETP
7. Variety of pine	HSCCTO

DOWN

CLUE	ANSWER
1. Symbolized by a fish	ECISPS
2. _____ Games	LYOCIPM
3. Give	REPESTN
4. Take	ANSHCT

CLUE: Ptolemaic queen

BONUS

How to play — Complete the crossword puzzle by looking at the clues and unscrambling the answers. When the puzzle is complete, unscramble the circled letters to solve the bonus.

PUZZLE

#52

JUMBLE CROSSWORDS™

ACROSS

CLUE	ANSWER
1. Check	RYEVIF
5. _____ story	ECRVO
6. Pointed wood	ASTEK
7. "Quickly," for example	DVBRAE

DOWN

CLUE	ANSWER
1. Emptiness of space	ACVMUU
2. Changed	EVRSIDE
3. Abandon	ROFASEK
4. Splendid	PESUBR

CLUE: H.M.'s mid-1800s creation

BONUS

How to play Complete the crossword puzzle by looking at the clues and unscrambling the answers. When the puzzle is complete, unscramble the circled letters to solve the bonus.

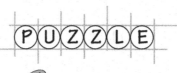

JUMBLE CROSSWORDS™

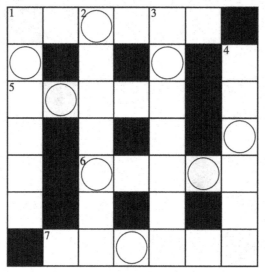

ACROSS

CLUE	ANSWER
1. Empty	N V T C A A
5. _____ food	L N T A P
6. Type of vessel	P B M I L
7. Deplorable	A R T C I G

DOWN

CLUE	ANSWER
1. Snakes	P V E S I R
2. Scramble	A R L C B E M
3. Zip	T I O G N H N
4. _____ of Cancer	R O C I P T

CLUE: One of the wettest inhabited places, Buenaventura (260 inches of rain each year), is in this country.

BONUS

How to play — Complete the crossword puzzle by looking at the clues and unscrambling the answers. When the puzzle is complete, unscramble the circled letters to solve the bonus.

#54

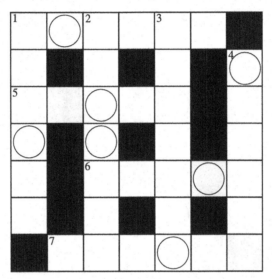

JUMBLE CROSSWORDS™

ACROSS

CLUE	ANSWER
1. Professional	PXETRE
5. _____ Sea	NHIAC
6. Hurts	HCASE
7. Tough band	ETNODN

DOWN

CLUE	ANSWER
1. Reason	XUSEEC
2. Mammal order	RIPAMET
3. Achieved	AERHCDE
4. Being	NPOESR

CLUE: ULDBJME

BONUS

How to play   Complete the crossword puzzle by looking at the clues and unscrambling the answers. When the puzzle is complete, unscramble the circled letters to solve the bonus.

PUZZLE #55

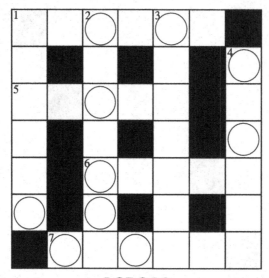

ACROSS

CLUE	ANSWER
1. Grumpy	BARCYB
5. L.R.'s TV pal	HTLEE
6. Give	DNWEO
7. Lean	AEREGM

DOWN

CLUE	ANSWER
1. Close tightly	ECCNHL
2. Baseball player, for example	HATEELT
3. Short-haired mammal	LGOUBDL
4. Solution	NESARW

BONUS **CLUE:** This is comprised of many islands.

How to play Complete the crossword puzzle by looking at the clues and unscrambling the answers. When the puzzle is complete, unscramble the circled letters to solve the bonus.

#56

JUMBLE CROSSWORDS™

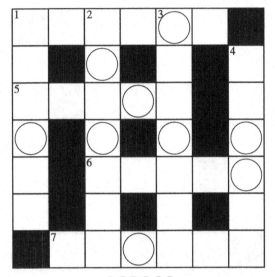

ACROSS

CLUE	ANSWER
1. Submerged	ENSKNU
5. _____ Bush	UAALR
6. Heavyset animal	NHIOR
7. Customer	ELITNC

DOWN

CLUE	ANSWER
1. _____ movie	LITNES
2. Indifferent	ULENRTA
3. Scrutinize	XEAEIMN
4. Gouge, squeeze	TXOTER

CLUE: Your odds of being hit by one are very slim.

BONUS ◯◯◯◯◯◯◯◯◯

How to play Complete the crossword puzzle by looking at the clues and unscrambling the answers. When the puzzle is complete, unscramble the circled letters to solve the bonus.

PUZZLE #57

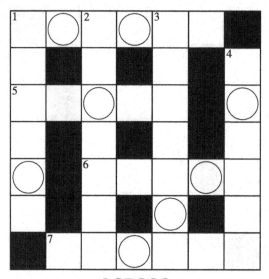

JUMBLE CROSSWORDS™

ACROSS

CLUE	ANSWER
1. Not spoken	NIDUAS
5. Gruesome	RLDIU
6. Collection of people	PORTO
7. Shaping tool	HLCEIS

DOWN

CLUE	ANSWER
1. Except	LNSEUS
2. Loosen up	TERSTHC
3. Inside	DNIROSO
4. Wedding _____	LEAHPC

CLUE: This U.S. president spent just 32 days in office.

BONUS

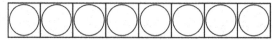

How to play Complete the crossword puzzle by looking at the clues and unscrambling the answers. When the puzzle is complete, unscramble the circled letters to solve the bonus.

PUZZLE

#58

JUMBLE CROSSWORDS™

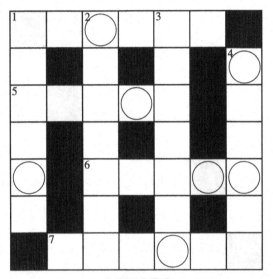

ACROSS

CLUE		ANSWER
1.	Baby _____	DRPWEO
5.	With	NOMGA
6.	Electric _____	PAOIN
7.	_____ shower	DLIRAB

DOWN

CLUE		ANSWER
1.	Hamper, burden	AGELPU
2.	Large falsehood	HRPOWEP
3.	New _____	LGNEDAN
4.	Walk	RTLOSL

CLUE: Type of ending

BONUS

How to play — Complete the crossword puzzle by looking at the clues and unscrambling the answers. When the puzzle is complete, unscramble the circled letters to solve the bonus.

PUZZLE #59

JUMBLE CROSSWORDS™

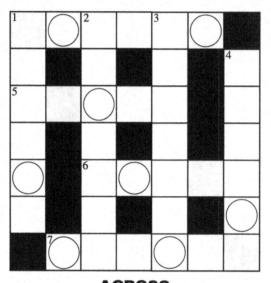

ACROSS

CLUE	ANSWER
1. Language	RJGANO
5. Matter	EISUS
6. Dipper	DALEL
7. Gems	LEESJW

DOWN

CLUE	ANSWER
1. Fluids	UEISJC
2. Work out	EVELOSR
3. Belated	DREUVEO
4. Arm muscles	PEISBC

CLUE: The _____ national anthem is just a few lines long.

BONUS

How to play — Complete the crossword puzzle by looking at the clues and unscrambling the answers. When the puzzle is complete, unscramble the circled letters to solve the bonus.

#60

JUMBLE CROSSWORDS™

ACROSS

CLUE	ANSWER
1. Alfred's boss	T B N A M A
5. While, bit, stretch	L P S L E
6. Eighth of its kind	H T A E T
7. Changed	D D T I E E

DOWN

CLUE	ANSWER
1. Hit	A E S D B H
2. Paid for	D T E R T A E
3. Infirmity	L I A E M T N
4. NATO member since '99	N A D P L O

CLUE: Home to Novosibirsk, Omsk, Krasnoyarsk, and Irkutsk.

BONUS

How to play — Complete the crossword puzzle by looking at the clues and unscrambling the answers. When the puzzle is complete, unscramble the circled letters to solve the bonus.

#61

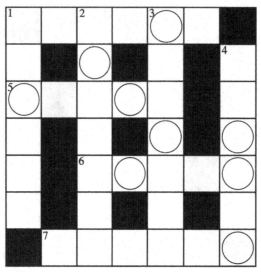

JUMBLE CROSSWORDS™

ACROSS

CLUE	ANSWER
1. Together	TNCITA
5. Out of place	MSIAS
6. Evade	ULEDE
7. Wise goddess	HATAEN

DOWN

CLUE	ANSWER
1. Son of Daedalus	ACISUR
2. Neptune's weapon	RITEDTN
3. Disguise	MOECUST
4. Rhizopod protozoan	AOEMAB

CLUE: Ocean Park, Hong Kong, is home to the world's longest _____.

BONUS

How to play   Complete the crossword puzzle by looking at the clues and unscrambling the answers. When the puzzle is complete, unscramble the circled letters to solve the bonus.

PUZZLE #62

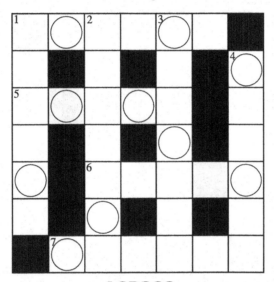

JUMBLE CROSSWORDS™

ACROSS

CLUE	ANSWER
1. Chicken	W D R A O C
5. Charon's partner	L O T U P
6. Legal right	R O D I T
7. American inventor	D I N S E O

DOWN

CLUE	ANSWER
1. Metallic element	P C R E P O
2. Hurt	U O W D D N E
3. Exuberant	T I O O R S U
4. To urge on	E H T S N A

BONUS CLUE: Common to all but one of the answers.

How to play — Complete the crossword puzzle by looking at the clues and unscrambling the answers. When the puzzle is complete, unscramble the circled letters to solve the bonus.

PUZZLE #63

JUMBLE CROSSWORDS™

ACROSS

CLUE	ANSWER
1. Steadfast	ATSELB
5. Rise	MLIBC
6. Past _____	EETSN
7. Cut	DUENRP

DOWN

CLUE	ANSWER
1. Eye _____	EOKTCS
2. Pilot	RIVOTAA
3. Cedar of _____	BEALONN
4. Filament	AHERDT

BONUS CLUE: "I just bought one after not owning one for 10 years." D.L.H.

How to play — Complete the crossword puzzle by looking at the clues and unscrambling the answers. When the puzzle is complete, unscramble the circled letters to solve the bonus.

#64

JUMBLE CROSSWORDS™

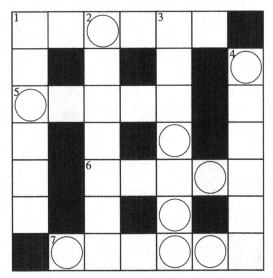

ACROSS

CLUE	ANSWER
1. Bad _____	PREEMT
5. _____ Reed	NODAN
6. Fibbing	YGNIL
7. Handsome man	DISAON

DOWN

CLUE	ANSWER
1. Boredom	DETMIU
2. Destroyed	NAMDELG
3. Happiness	ANLEITO
4. Moves	DUBSEG

CLUE: An official Olympic sport since 1992.

BONUS

How to play   Complete the crossword puzzle by looking at the clues and unscrambling the answers. When the puzzle is complete, unscramble the circled letters to solve the bonus.

JUMBLE CROSSWORDS™

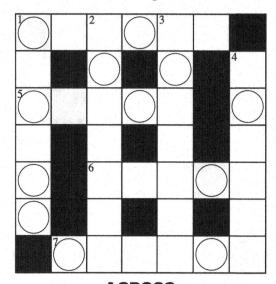

ACROSS

CLUE	ANSWER
1. A country capital	T O A T A W
5. Type of meal	A E T S F
6. Wield	E E R X T
7. Rationale	A S N R E O

DOWN

CLUE	ANSWER
1. Transgress	D F O E F N
2. _____ artist	Z R A T E P E
3. 1985 movie	T S I W E N S
4. Small energy unit	H T O N O P

CLUE: This popular actor, who shares his last name with
BONUS   a former political leader, doesn't have a middle name.

How to play   Complete the crossword puzzle by looking at the clues and
unscrambling the answers. When the puzzle is complete,
unscramble the circled letters to solve the bonus.

JUMBLE CROSSWORDS™

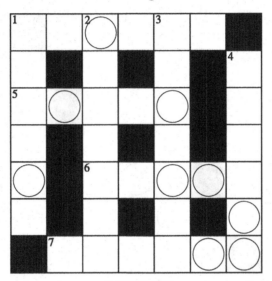

ACROSS

CLUE	ANSWER
1. South American city	A B T O O G
5. French _____	C N R A F
6. Cherish	Z I P E R
7. _____ plan	O E S N L S

DOWN

CLUE	ANSWER
1. Batter	F B U T E F
2. Wrestle	P A R G E L P
3. Strategies	S T A C C I T
4. Vascular organ	E S E N L P

CLUE: Know

BONUS

How to play — Complete the crossword puzzle by looking at the clues and unscrambling the answers. When the puzzle is complete, unscramble the circled letters to solve the bonus.

PUZZLE #67

JUMBLE CROSSWORDS™

ACROSS

CLUE	ANSWER
1. Drivel	ELBBBA
5. Pains' partner	HSECA
6. Encounters	TMSEE
7. Transferred	AESDPS

DOWN

CLUE	ANSWER
1. Holder	AEBRRE
2. Czech region	HOIBMEA
3. Heeds	NIESTSL
4. Damned	RUCDES

CLUE: Armenia and Azerbaijan

BONUS ◯◯◯◯◯◯◯◯◯

How to play — Complete the crossword puzzle by looking at the clues and unscrambling the answers. When the puzzle is complete, unscramble the circled letters to solve the bonus.

#68

JUMBLE CROSSWORDS™

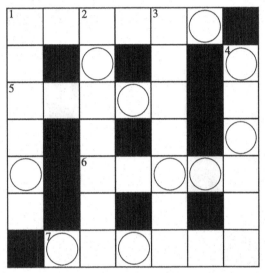

ACROSS

CLUE	ANSWER
1. Simply	A S E Y I L
5. Decree	N A C N O
6. "Off your _____"	U O G D R
7. Shoulder _____	D A L E B S

DOWN

CLUE	ANSWER
1. Energize	X T I C E E
2. African nation	N E S G E L A
3. Drooping	D I N L U A G
4. Crowds	R E O S H D

BONUS **CLUE:** Even though this is very light,
you can't hold it for very long.

How to play   Complete the crossword puzzle by looking at the clues and unscrambling the answers. When the puzzle is complete, unscramble the circled letters to solve the bonus.

69

JUMBLE CROSSWORDS™

ACROSS

CLUE	ANSWER
1. Total	TUANMO
5. Blunder	FGFEA
6. Baby condition	LCIOC
7. Sports transactions	ARTSED

DOWN

CLUE	ANSWER
1. Home to Luanda	NOAGAL
2. Petty _____	FIFRECO
3. Pestered	ENDEELD
4. Pants	LSCASK

BONUS   **CLUE:** "Laurel" and "Hardy"

How to play   Complete the crossword puzzle by looking at the clues and unscrambling the answers. When the puzzle is complete, unscramble the circled letters to solve the bonus.

JUMBLE CROSSWORDS™

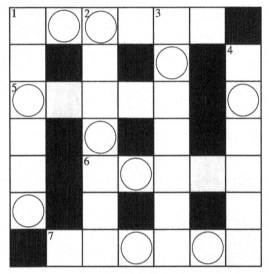

ACROSS

CLUE		ANSWER
1.	Sunken area	UUTDOG
5.	Drawing _____	BADRO
6.	Be present at the arrival of	TEMSE
7.	Of inferior quality	ARTHYS

DOWN

CLUE		ANSWER
1.	A large city	BUDNIL
2.	_____ school	RAMRMAG
3.	Disrobe	NSDUERS
4.	Mess	TIYPSG

BONUS   **CLUE:** Man or woman

How to play   Complete the crossword puzzle by looking at the clues and unscrambling the answers. When the puzzle is complete, unscramble the circled letters to solve the bonus.

PUZZLE #71

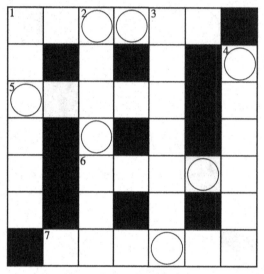

JUMBLE CROSSWORDS™

ACROSS

CLUE	ANSWER
1. Maximum	MTUOTS
5. Asian animal	DAAPN
6. Olive family member	LLAIC
7. Beautifies	RDNOAS

DOWN

CLUE	ANSWER
1. Judge	RMUEIP
2. Mixed	NDIMLGE
3. Fastener	ERTSLAP
4. Responds	AERSTC

CLUE: Show

BONUS

How to play — Complete the crossword puzzle by looking at the clues and unscrambling the answers. When the puzzle is complete, unscramble the circled letters to solve the bonus.

JUMBLE CROSSWORDS™

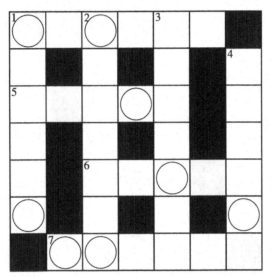

ACROSS

CLUE	ANSWER
1. Entry	ASCSEC
5. Congaree _____	MWPAS
6. Rings	PHSOO
7. Stick	HDEEAR

DOWN

CLUE	ANSWER
1. Monopolize	BSBROA
2. Fought	DCEHASL
3. Reckon	PSOPESU
4. Long-running TV show	AIELSS

CLUE: Home to about 13 million people.

BONUS

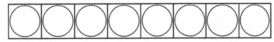

How to play — Complete the crossword puzzle by looking at the clues and unscrambling the answers. When the puzzle is complete, unscramble the circled letters to solve the bonus.

JUMBLE CROSSWORDS™

ACROSS

CLUE	ANSWER
1. Disappointment	M I D Y S A
5. Shun	D I A O V
6. Improve	N D M A E
7. Aspects	H A P S E S

DOWN

CLUE	ANSWER
1. Serpent	A D G N O R
2. Handle	T O S A M H C
3. Point toward	R D S E A S D
4. Razor _____	L B S D A E

CLUE: This product first appeared in 1921.

BONUS  -

How to play   Complete the crossword puzzle by looking at the clues and unscrambling the answers. When the puzzle is complete, unscramble the circled letters to solve the bonus.

#74

JUMBLE CROSSWORDS™

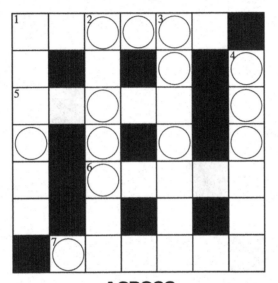

ACROSS

CLUE	ANSWER
1. Irregular	N N E E U V
5. Disorder	A O V H C
6. Wingless form	R A L A V
7. Sporadic	T P S O Y T

DOWN

CLUE	ANSWER
1. Difficult	L P I H L U
2. To swathe	E L O N P E V
3. Brief portion	R C P E E T X
4. Evil reputation	N M Y I A F

CLUE: Unscramble the circled letters to make a correct math equation.

◯◯◯ + ◯◯◯◯ = ◯◯◯◯◯◯◯

How to play   Complete the crossword puzzle by looking at the clues and unscrambling the answers. When the puzzle is complete, unscramble the circled letters to solve the bonus.

JUMBLE CROSSWORDS™

ACROSS

CLUE	ANSWER
1. Fire _____	N E N E I G
5. Stuck	L C G U N
6. Combine	R E E G M
7. Reach	N T T I A A

DOWN

CLUE	ANSWER
1. Depart	A E E S C P
2. Epicure	U G M R T E O
3. Neighbor to Cameroon	N R I G I E A
4. Fresh	E D R O N M

CLUE: Dear

BONUS

How to play — Complete the crossword puzzle by looking at the clues and unscrambling the answers. When the puzzle is complete, unscramble the circled letters to solve the bonus.

#76

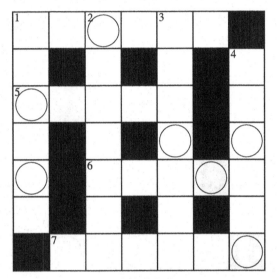

JUMBLE CROSSWORDS ™

ACROSS

CLUE	ANSWER
1. Colombian capital	T G A O B O
5. Split	L H E V A
6. Ghastly	R L I U D
7. Allocate	M I C M O T

DOWN

CLUE	ANSWER
1. Subsequent to	N I H D E B
2. Historical Italian	L G L O E I A
3. Principle	H E T R O M E
4. Critic	N U P T I D

CLUE: "You'll win this if you can solve this puzzle in under one minute." D.L.H.

BONUS

How to play   Complete the crossword puzzle by looking at the clues and unscrambling the answers. When the puzzle is complete, unscramble the circled letters to solve the bonus.

PUZZLE

#77

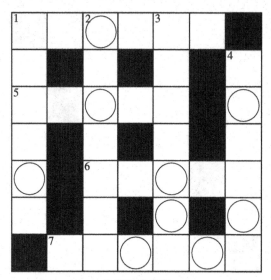

JUMBLE CROSSWORDS™

ACROSS

CLUE	ANSWER
1. Heart	KTCIRE
5. Short, sharp sound	RHIPC
6. In a frenzied state	MACKU
7. Instant	NMMTEO

DOWN

CLUE	ANSWER
1. Amuse	ETLIKC
2. Large U.S. city	HICCOGA
3. Support	PSEUOES
4. _____ seat	UKTBCE

CLUE: Small

BONUS ○○○○○○○○○

How to play — Complete the crossword puzzle by looking at the clues and unscrambling the answers. When the puzzle is complete, unscramble the circled letters to solve the bonus.

PUZZLE #78

JUMBLE CROSSWORDS™

CLUE: Upside down

ACROSS

CLUE	ANSWER
1. Open	RWANPU
5. Jeopardy	LEPIR
6. Red	TRLEA
7. Rankle ___	FTRESE

DOWN

CLUE	ANSWER
1. Judge	PMURIE
2. Conflict	RAWAFER
3. Disorder	LIAEMTN
4. Witch ___	RCOOTD

BONUS

How to play — Complete the crossword puzzle by looking at the clues and unscrambling the answers. When the puzzle is complete, unscramble the circled letters to solve the bonus.

#79

JUMBLE CROSSWORDS™

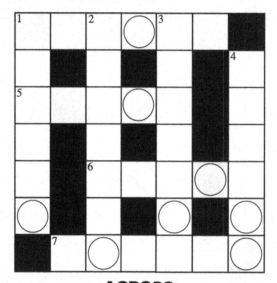

ACROSS

CLUE	ANSWER
1. A common currency	L R O D A L
5. Sure _____	N H I T G
6. Association	U N N I O
7. Fatal	T E L L A H

DOWN

CLUE	ANSWER
1. Loathe	T D T S E E
2. Ease, freedom	E E L U S I R
3. Heartache	N U S H A I G
4. Indication	L I A S G N

CLUE: Some paintings by this actor have sold for more than $40,000.

BONUS

How to play   Complete the crossword puzzle by looking at the clues and unscrambling the answers. When the puzzle is complete, unscramble the circled letters to solve the bonus.

JUMBLE CROSSWORDS™

ACROSS

CLUE	ANSWER
1. Legendary rider	DGOIAV
5. Emergency _____	ARBEK
6. Feeling	HHNUC
7. Full	MAJDEM

DOWN

CLUE	ANSWER
1. Drinking vessel	BOGTEL
2. Ancient unit	ARDHCAM
3. Neighbor to China	ENITMAV
4. Crushed	DMSEHA

BONUS

CLUE: Bold and beautiful

How to play   Complete the crossword puzzle by looking at the clues and unscrambling the answers. When the puzzle is complete, unscramble the circled letters to solve the bonus.

81

JUMBLE CROSSWORDS™

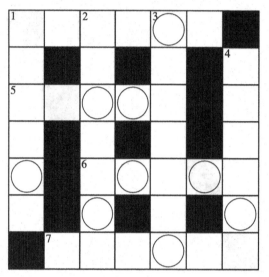

ACROSS

CLUE	ANSWER
1. Water rider	FRUSER
5. Bulbous herb	LIUTP
6. Mysterious	RIEEE
7. A large city	BTUEIR

DOWN

CLUE	ANSWER
1. Type of fiber	TUSEUR
2. Mitigate	LVERIEE
3. Ruler	PMREERO
4. Strong	NOETTP

BONUS **CLUE:** This is about 3,500 miles long.

THE

How to play   Complete the crossword puzzle by looking at the clues and unscrambling the answers. When the puzzle is complete, unscramble the circled letters to solve the bonus.

#82

JUMBLE CROSSWORDS™

ACROSS

CLUE	ANSWER
1. Break	THAISU
5. _____ Beach	AIMIM
6. Smug look	RSIKM
7. Least normal	DOTSED

DOWN

CLUE	ANSWER
1. Tribute	EOGHAM
2. Collected	AADESMS
3. Producing togetherness	NIUITEV
4. Small parcel	CAKPTE

CLUE: This instrument was invented in 1821.

BONUS

How to play   Complete the crossword puzzle by looking at the clues and unscrambling the answers. When the puzzle is complete, unscramble the circled letters to solve the bonus.

PUZZLE #83

JUMBLE CROSSWORDS™

ACROSS

CLUE	ANSWER
1. Travel _____	EGCNAY
5. Jupiter, for example	TIHFF
6. Furious	BRDIA
7. Tea _____	LTEETK

DOWN

CLUE	ANSWER
1. Love _____	FRIFAA
2. Compel, constrain	ROFCNEE
3. Live together	HOICBAT
4. Promise	GEEDLP

BONUS

CLUE: Animal depository

How to play — Complete the crossword puzzle by looking at the clues and unscrambling the answers. When the puzzle is complete, unscramble the circled letters to solve the bonus.

PUZZLE

#84

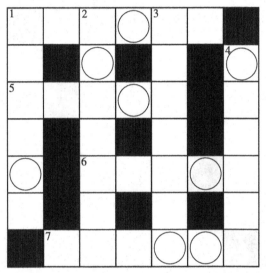

JUMBLE CROSSWORDS™

ACROSS

CLUE	ANSWER
1. Fight	B E L U R M
5. City in Iraq	A A R S B
6. Resource	T S A E S
7. Plan	D E G A A N

DOWN

CLUE	ANSWER
1. Type of disease	B I A R S E
2. Horse or car	U G S M A T N
3. Affair	A I L S I N O
4. G.W.'s spouse	R A T M A H

CLUE: In the 1400s, the first homes to be _____ were in Paris.

BONUS

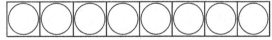

How to play   Complete the crossword puzzle by looking at the clues and unscrambling the answers. When the puzzle is complete, unscramble the circled letters to solve the bonus.

85

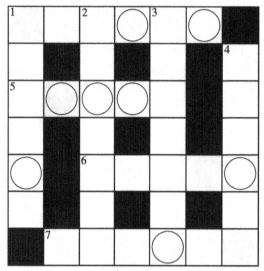

JUMBLE CROSSWORDS™

ACROSS

CLUE	ANSWER
1. Implement	NKOVIE
5. Type of feline	BABTY
6. Ancient Greek dialect	TCIAT
7. Slanted	LAEEDN

DOWN

CLUE	ANSWER
1. _____ valve	TNIKEA
2. Shake	ATIRBVE
3. C.K.'s birthplace	ROTPYKN
4. Calm	ALDICP

CLUE: The giant squid is the largest creature without a _____.

BONUS

 How to play — Complete the crossword puzzle by looking at the clues and unscrambling the answers. When the puzzle is complete, unscramble the circled letters to solve the bonus.

JUMBLE CROSSWORDS™

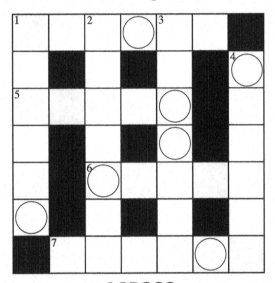

ACROSS

CLUE	ANSWER
1. Constructed	D F E O M R
5. Wash	H T A B E
6. Smell	A A M O R
7. Blue _____	E R S T K A

DOWN

CLUE	ANSWER
1. Lied	B F D E I B
2. Withdraw	T E R A R T C
3. Unattractive sight	E E E R O S Y
4. Reveal	M N K A U S

CLUE: 1984 "Best Picture"

BONUS

How to play   Complete the crossword puzzle by looking at the clues and unscrambling the answers. When the puzzle is complete, unscramble the circled letters to solve the bonus.

PUZZLE #87

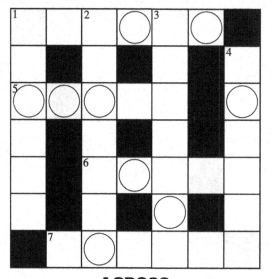

JUMBLE CROSSWORDS™

ACROSS

CLUE	ANSWER
1. _____ Peninsula	LABNAK
5. Terra-_____	TCOAT
6. Dangerous	KISYR
7. Ooze	DSEGUL

DOWN

CLUE	ANSWER
1. Summon	ECBNOK
2. Actual	TILLREA
3. Assembled	MAADESS
4. Complex protein	ZEEMNY

CLUE: George Lucas considered this actor for the role of Han Solo in "Star Wars."

BONUS

⬡⬡⬡⬡   ⬡⬡⬡⬡⬡

How to play — Complete the crossword puzzle by looking at the clues and unscrambling the answers. When the puzzle is complete, unscramble the circled letters to solve the bonus.

PUZZLE

#88

JUMBLE CROSSWORDS™

ACROSS

CLUE	ANSWER
1. Gloomy	ARDERY
5. Luxury	LFIRL
6. Wield	RXEET
7. Sea _____	TRSEOT

DOWN

CLUE	ANSWER
1. Mar	FAEDEC
2. Clear	TNVEEID
3. Allay	LEREEIV
4. Cooking frames	ARGSET

CLUE: The state of Washington's official state insect.

BONUS

How to play — Complete the crossword puzzle by looking at the clues and unscrambling the answers. When the puzzle is complete, unscramble the circled letters to solve the bonus.

JUMBLE CROSSWORDS™

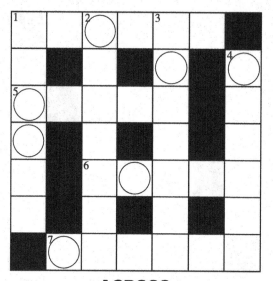

ACROSS

CLUE	ANSWER
1. Representative part	PMEASL
5. Accepted rule	NNOAC
6. 1979 movie	AILNE
7. Short-legged mammal	EEGBLA

DOWN

CLUE	ANSWER
1. Confident	RCSEEU
2. Commonplace	NADUENM
3. Wanting	LNGIGNO
4. _____ tree	RAOEGN

CLUE: This TV show debuted in 1968.

BONUS

How to play — Complete the crossword puzzle by looking at the clues and unscrambling the answers. When the puzzle is complete, unscramble the circled letters to solve the bonus.

#90

JUMBLE CROSSWORDS™

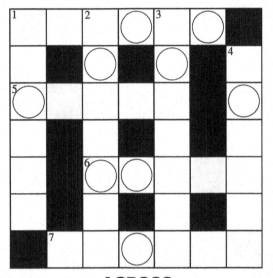

ACROSS

CLUE	ANSWER
1. Ground _____	P P P R E E
5. Group of islands	L A M A T
6. Studied, inspected	E A S C D
7. Dull	D T O Y G S

DOWN

CLUE	ANSWER
1. Beat	M L U P E M
2. Carnivorous mammal	L P C E T A O
3. Passed	A S D L E P E
4. Affectionately	N L Y D O F

CLUE: This man shares his last name with a game.

BONUS

How to play — Complete the crossword puzzle by looking at the clues and unscrambling the answers. When the puzzle is complete, unscramble the circled letters to solve the bonus.

PUZZLE #91

JUMBLE CROSSWORDS™

ACROSS

CLUE	ANSWER
1. Plan	MHEECS
5. Home to New Delhi	DINIA
6. Sharp	UACET
7. Affirm	TAETTS

DOWN

CLUE	ANSWER
1. Repress	FTISLE
2. Discharge pipe	DYHARTN
3. _____ up	REMEUAS
4. Instant	MNMEOT

BONUS CLUE: This country once had two official national anthems.

How to play — Complete the crossword puzzle by looking at the clues and unscrambling the answers. When the puzzle is complete, unscramble the circled letters to solve the bonus.

#92

JUMBLE CROSSWORDS™

ACROSS

CLUE	ANSWER
1. Injury	UMRAAT
5. Martian	NAIEL
6. Needle	TESAE
7. Erratic	RTNARE

DOWN

CLUE	ANSWER
1. Lamentable	ARTCIG
2. Airplane controller	TIAROVA
3. Joe _____	NOAATNM
4. Doppler _____	FCETEF

CLUE: No two are the same.

BONUS

How to play   Complete the crossword puzzle by looking at the clues and unscrambling the answers. When the puzzle is complete, unscramble the circled letters to solve the bonus.

PUZZLE #93

JUMBLE CROSSWORDS™

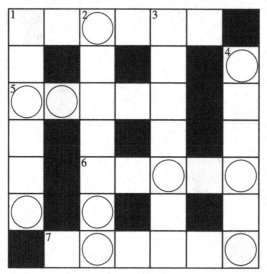

ACROSS

CLUE	ANSWER
1. Relax	WNIUDN
5. Extent	LEAMR
6. Robbery	ESTIH
7. Weak and unsteady	YORGGG

DOWN

CLUE	ANSWER
1. Turmoil	RNUSET
2. _____ map	AEWHTRE
3. Desensitizing	MGNUIBN
4. _____ chef	PSYTAR

BONUS **CLUE:** Charles Thurber received a patent on an early one in 1843.

How to play — Complete the crossword puzzle by looking at the clues and unscrambling the answers. When the puzzle is complete, unscramble the circled letters to solve the bonus.

#94

JUMBLE CROSSWORDS™

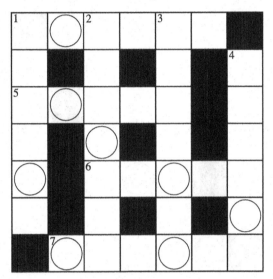

ACROSS

CLUE	ANSWER
1. Assert	FRMAIF
5. Projecting part	RNGPO
6. 820-mile river	ERNIH
7. Slowly or quickly	REDBAV

DOWN

CLUE	ANSWER
1. Angle	PSATCE
2. Shocked	LOFODER
3. Musical style	AMERIGT
4. Splendid	PSBREU

CLUE: The U.S. _____ _____
was formed in the forties.

BONUS ○○○ ○○○○○

How to play Complete the crossword puzzle by looking at the clues and unscrambling the answers. When the puzzle is complete, unscramble the circled letters to solve the bonus.

PUZZLE #95

JUMBLE CROSSWORDS™

ACROSS

CLUE	ANSWER
1. Find	L E O T A C
5. Thin porridge	R L E U G
6. Unschooled	E I A V N
7. Thomas _____	D O E I N S

DOWN

CLUE	ANSWER
1. Smooth manner	E G L T A O
2. Agitated	H U C N R D E
3. Calculates	L E A T I L S
4. _____ test	N E C S E R

CLUE: Land

BONUS

How to play Complete the crossword puzzle by looking at the clues and unscrambling the answers. When the puzzle is complete, unscramble the circled letters to solve the bonus.

#96

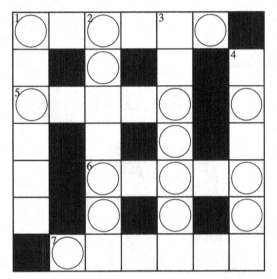

JUMBLE CROSSWORDS™

ACROSS

CLUE	ANSWER
1. European city	A A W S R W
5. Banquet	T E S F A
6. Taut	H G I T T
7. Elaborate	N R O E A T

DOWN

CLUE	ANSWER
1. _____ cone	F E A W L F
2. Agent	E R T L R O A
3. Home to St. John's	G N A U A I T
4. Detest	L H O E T A

CLUE: Unscramble the circled letters to make a correct math equation.

BONUS

How to play — Complete the crossword puzzle by looking at the clues and unscrambling the answers. When the puzzle is complete, unscramble the circled letters to solve the bonus.

PUZZLE

 #97

JUMBLE CROSSWORDS™

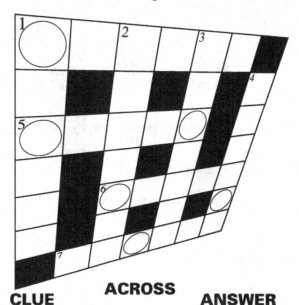

CLUE — **ACROSS** — **ANSWER**

1. Fall — LGUPEN
5. Oscar _____ — DIWEL
6. Moderate — TABAE
7. Group of words — RESAPH

CLUE — **DOWN** — **ANSWER**

1. Type of alloy — WERETP
2. Release — LNUAEHS
3. West Indies island — AADNGRE
4. Hinder — DMEEIP

CLUE: Puzzle grid adjective

BONUS

How to play — Complete the crossword puzzle by looking at the clues and unscrambling the answers. When the puzzle is complete, unscramble the circled letters to solve the bonus.

#98

JUMBLE CROSSWORDS™

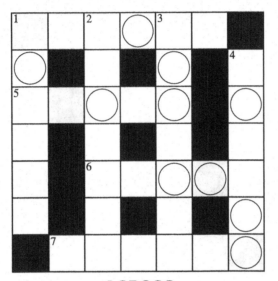

ACROSS

CLUE	ANSWER
1. Boll _____	L W I V E E
5. Teacher of Aristotle	T O A L P
6. _____ sign	E E C A P
7. Beat	F T E D A E

DOWN

CLUE	ANSWER
1. Windshield _____	P I E W S R
2. Paradigm	M A E E P L X
3. Separate	L O S I E T A
4. _____ of truth	T M M E O N

BONUS   **CLUE:** A leading exporter of lobster.

How to play   Complete the crossword puzzle by looking at the clues and unscrambling the answers. When the puzzle is complete, unscramble the circled letters to solve the bonus.

#99

JUMBLE CROSSWORDS™

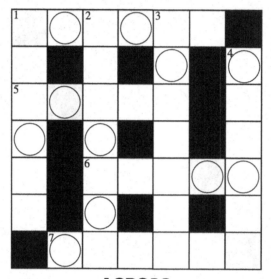

ACROSS

CLUE	ANSWER
1. Newspaper section	M C I S O C
5. _____ tree	E L O M N
6. Approaches	A E N S R
7. Shocked	T O D L E J

DOWN

CLUE	ANSWER
1. Unemotionally	L L C Y D O
2. Relic	T O M M N E E
3. 1997 movie	N C O C A T T
4. Bickered	U S D F S E

BONUS CLUE: This actress was George Lucas' original choice to play Princess Leia in "Star Wars."

○ ○ ○ ○ ○   ○ ○ ○ ○ ○ ○ ○

How to play Complete the crossword puzzle by looking at the clues and unscrambling the answers. When the puzzle is complete, unscramble the circled letters to solve the bonus.

#100

JUMBLE CROSSWORDS™

ACROSS

CLUE	ANSWER
1. Signaling device	Z U R E Z B
5. Smooth	U A E S V
6. Performer	T C A R O
7. Loves	R O D S E A

DOWN

CLUE	ANSWER
1. Chess piece	P I H O S B
2. New _____	A L N A E Z D
3. _____ set	R E E T C R O
4. _____ wheel	F S I R R E

CLUE: People

BONUS

How to play   Complete the crossword puzzle by looking at the clues and unscrambling the answers. When the puzzle is complete, unscramble the circled letters to solve the bonus.

PUZZLE

#101

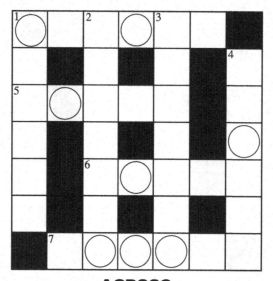

JUMBLE CROSSWORDS™

ACROSS

CLUE	ANSWER
1. Burn	HRCCSO
5. Group	TCOTE
6. Large Japanese port	AOKAS
7. Water _____	KRIESS

DOWN

CLUE	ANSWER
1. Even	MOSHOT
2. Forecast	KTOOOUL
3. Small dwelling	ETATGOC
4. Waterways	NACSLA

CLUE: This candy bar was introduced in 1930.

BONUS

How to play — Complete the crossword puzzle by looking at the clues and unscrambling the answers. When the puzzle is complete, unscramble the circled letters to solve the bonus.

JUMBLE® CROSSWORDS™

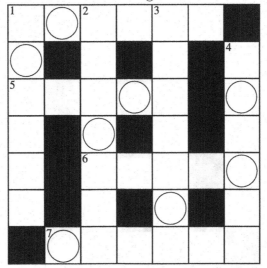

ACROSS

CLUE	ANSWER
1. Outline	E A G N A D
5. Damp	T M S I O
6. Different	H T O R E
7. Sell	D E E L D P

DOWN

CLUE	ANSWER
1. Large force	M R A D A A
2. Show	P I E O S E D
3. Discarded	T D H C D I E
4. Rough, coarse	A O R H E S

CLUE: Humans' "unstoppable" movement

BONUS

How to play — Complete the crossword puzzle by looking at the clues and unscrambling the answers. When the puzzle is complete, unscramble the circled letters to solve the bonus.

PUZZLE #103

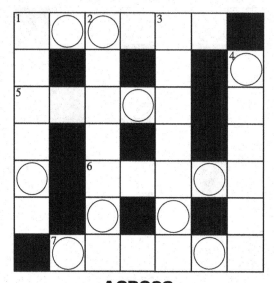

ACROSS

CLUE	ANSWER
1. Concoction	N O O I T P
5. Thud	M H P T U
6. Reside	W L D E L
7. Stopped	E E S A D C

DOWN

CLUE	ANSWER
1. Type of club	T P R E T U
2. _____ bed	R L E U T D N
3. Burden by abuse	P S O S R E P
4. Eliminated	L I K D E L

CLUE: This popular actor appeared on a 1968 episode of *The Dating Game.*

BONUS

How to play — Complete the crossword puzzle by looking at the clues and unscrambling the answers. When the puzzle is complete, unscramble the circled letters to solve the bonus.

#104

JUMBLE CROSSWORDS™

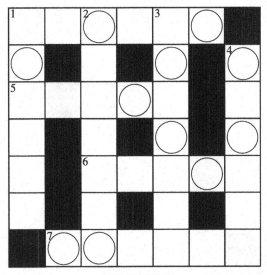

ACROSS

CLUE	ANSWER
1. Flat slab	BTELAT
5. Faux pas	RRROE
6. Nahuatl speaker	TZACE
7. Light meals	NAKCSS

DOWN

CLUE	ANSWER
1. Quantum _____	EHTROY
2. Deal	RABAGIN
3. Inconsistent	TARIRCE
4. Ruins	KRSWCE

BONUS CLUE: This man mortgaged his house to finance his second edition.

How to play   Complete the crossword puzzle by looking at the clues and unscrambling the answers. When the puzzle is complete, unscramble the circled letters to solve the bonus.

PUZZLE #105

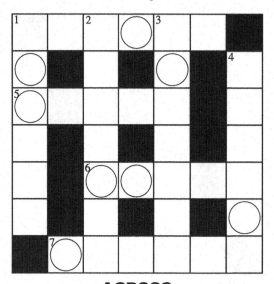

ACROSS

CLUE		ANSWER
1.	Victor	NREIWN
5.	Live	TXSIE
6.	_____ Plateau	ZKRAO
7.	_____ engine	LIDEES

DOWN

CLUE		ANSWER
1.	Downhearted	ELOWUF
2.	A country capital	AINORIB
3.	Captures	TENARSP
4.	Metallic element	KEICLN

CLUE: (1 + 2) x 6 - (3 + 3) =

How to play — Complete the crossword puzzle by looking at the clues and unscrambling the answers. When the puzzle is complete, unscramble the circled letters to solve the bonus.

JUMBLE CROSSWORDS™

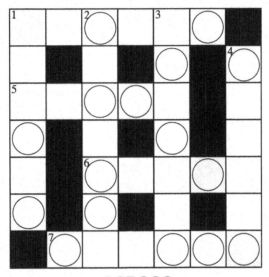

ACROSS

CLUE	ANSWER
1. Heritage	LYCEAG
5. Town _____	ERIRC
6. 13 through 19	NTESE
7. Foamy	HRYFTO

DOWN

CLUE	ANSWER
1. Type of insect	TLSOUC
2. Sparkling objects	LIGRTTE
3. Amend	RCERTOC
4. Potent drink	KHIWYS

BONUS

CLUE: Unscramble the circled letters to make a correct math equation.

○○○○○○ X ○○○○ = ○○○○○○

How to play — Complete the crossword puzzle by looking at the clues and unscrambling the answers. When the puzzle is complete, unscramble the circled letters to solve the bonus.

JUMBLE® CROSSWORDS™

ACROSS

CLUE	ANSWER
1. Expose	M K N U S A
5. Depressed	N L F R O O R
6. Reminders	T O S E N
7. Terrified	R A C E D S

DOWN

CLUE	ANSWER
1. Inequitable	F A N I R U
2. Dumb	R O I M N C O
3. Marksman	H S R T O O E
4. New	D E N S U U

BONUS   **CLUE:** Strange

How to play   Complete the crossword puzzle by looking at the clues and unscrambling the answers. When the puzzle is complete, unscramble the circled letters to solve the bonus.

#108

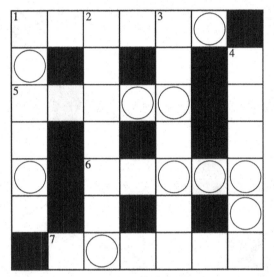

JUMBLE CROSSWORDS™

ACROSS

CLUE	ANSWER
1. Game plan	HSCMEE
5. Georgia city	NMAOC
6. Broad cloth	RCAFS
7. Candies	WTESES

DOWN

CLUE	ANSWER
1. _____ interest	MSELIP
2. Cutting instrument	ACWHSKA
3. Prosaic	NEMADNU
4. Jams	TFSFSU

BONUS   **CLUE:** This was invented in 1869.

How to play   Complete the crossword puzzle by looking at the clues and unscrambling the answers. When the puzzle is complete, unscramble the circled letters to solve the bonus.

JUMBLE CROSSWORDS™

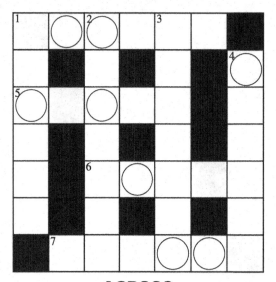

ACROSS

CLUE	ANSWER
1. Secret	ROEVTC
5. Grasping devices	NSOTG
6. Combine	TINEU
7. Spot	EETDTC

DOWN

CLUE	ANSWER
1. _____ fruit	RTICSU
2. Enterprise	EVREUTN
3. Break	PSIEERT
4. Missing	BNTAES

CLUE: Contract

BONUS

How to play — Complete the crossword puzzle by looking at the clues and unscrambling the answers. When the puzzle is complete, unscramble the circled letters to solve the bonus.

JUMBLE® CROSSWORDS™

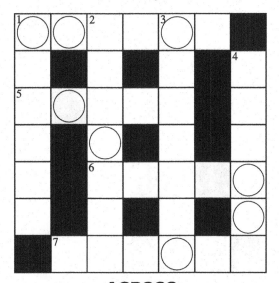

ACROSS

CLUE	ANSWER
1. Large feline	A A U G R J
5. Openings	L T I S S
6. Deserve	M E T I R
7. Dismal	E R D Y R A

DOWN

CLUE	ANSWER
1. Agitate	L O E J T S
2. Inkling	E I L M R G M
3. Freud home	U I A A R T S
4. Vile	L Y I F H T

CLUE: Planes are not allowed to fly over the _____ _____.

 **BONUS** ○○○ ○○○○○

How to play — Complete the crossword puzzle by looking at the clues and unscrambling the answers. When the puzzle is complete, unscramble the circled letters to solve the bonus.

JUMBLE CROSSWORDS™

ACROSS

CLUE   **ANSWER**

1. Small piece   ROMLES
5. Accumulate   AHROD
6. High school students   ENSET
7. Secure   URTYTS

DOWN

CLUE   **ANSWER**

1. _____ Indians   HOMKWA
2. Atomic _____   AERTCRO
3. Indefinite   DLSNEES
4. Irritable, dour   URCTYS

CLUE: This is comprised of about 65 percent water.

BONUS

How to play   Complete the crossword puzzle by looking at the clues and unscrambling the answers. When the puzzle is complete, unscramble the circled letters to solve the bonus.

#112

JUMBLE CROSSWORDS™

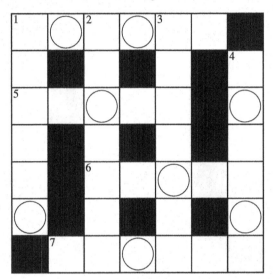

ACROSS

CLUE	ANSWER
1. Accomplish	TANTIA
5. Zest	UTGOS
6. Flattens	RNIOS
7. Exit	ESERGS

DOWN

CLUE	ANSWER
1. Yearly time period	TUUGAS
2. Wine _____	ASTGITN
3. Carbon-14, for example	POEIOTS
4. Lyrics	RSVSEE

CLUE: This creature has very dense fur (up to one million hairs per square inch).

BONUS

How to play   Complete the crossword puzzle by looking at the clues and unscrambling the answers. When the puzzle is complete, unscramble the circled letters to solve the bonus.

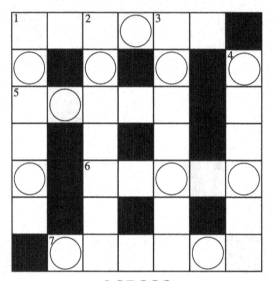

JUMBLE CROSSWORDS™

ACROSS

CLUE	ANSWER
1. Enough	EYLPNT
5. _____ powder	LIHIC
6. Up to such time as	NLIUT
7. You, to these words	ARERED

DOWN

CLUE	ANSWER
1. Ready to leave	ACPDEK
2. Gourmet	PIEUCER
3. Corrupted	DATETIN
4. Automated _____	RLLTEE

BONUS

CLUE: Home

 How to play — Complete the crossword puzzle by looking at the clues and unscrambling the answers. When the puzzle is complete, unscramble the circled letters to solve the bonus.

JUMBLE CROSSWORDS™

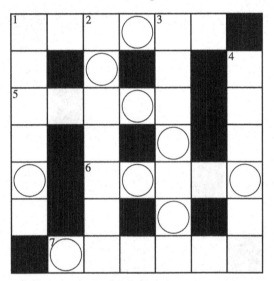

ACROSS

CLUE	ANSWER
1. Cushioned	D P E D D A
5. Matter	U S E I S
6. Last Greek letter	M A G E O
7. Fevered	T C I E C H

DOWN

CLUE	ANSWER
1. Moldable	L I P T N A
2. Undress	B I E D O R S
3. "H" or "O"	T E E E M N L
4. Composite	M C I O A S

BONUS

CLUE: A noologist studies this.

How to play — Complete the crossword puzzle by looking at the clues and unscrambling the answers. When the puzzle is complete, unscramble the circled letters to solve the bonus.

#115

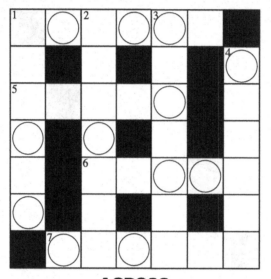

ACROSS

CLUE	ANSWER
1. Elfish person	PTIRSE
5. Insect eater	EOKCG
6. _____ hand	PREPU
7. Holder	REREBA

DOWN

CLUE	ANSWER
1. Traffic _____	NISLAG
2. Brown _____ spider	ECRULES
3. Good sport	ROTPORE
4. Closer	AENRRE

BONUS   CLUE: A 1938 invention.

How to play   Complete the crossword puzzle by looking at the clues and unscrambling the answers. When the puzzle is complete, unscramble the circled letters to solve the bonus.

#116

JUMBLE CROSSWORDS™

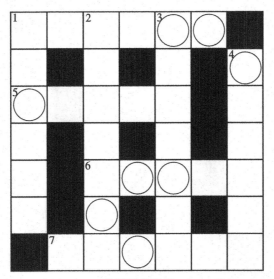

ACROSS

CLUE	ANSWER
1. The sixth-largest of its kind	REOEPU
5. Disturbance	TMROS
6. Signed	NKIDE
7. _____ soda	AGNREO

DOWN

CLUE	ANSWER
1. Follows	UNSSEE
2. More spacious	MIOERRO
3. _____ seeds	NIKMPPU
4. Roman _____	ACELDN

CLUE: Joint protectors

BONUS

How to play — Complete the crossword puzzle by looking at the clues and unscrambling the answers. When the puzzle is complete, unscramble the circled letters to solve the bonus.

PUZZLE

#117

JUMBLE CROSSWORDS™

ACROSS

CLUE	ANSWER
1. Interweave	LPSIEC
5. Claude _____	MNOTE
6. Dodge	AEDVE
7. In _____	NIUSNO

DOWN

CLUE	ANSWER
1. Peace _____	MYSLOB
2. Chinese _____	ATNELNR
3. Curved weapon	TSUCALS
4. Natural chamber	RAENCV

BONUS **CLUE:** More men are this than women.

◯◯◯◯ — ◯◯◯◯◯

How to play Complete the crossword puzzle by looking at the clues and unscrambling the answers. When the puzzle is complete, unscramble the circled letters to solve the bonus.

#118

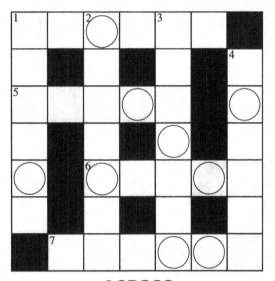

ACROSS

CLUE	ANSWER
1. Diesel _____	N G N I E E
5. Impassive	T C I O S
6. Assists the sheriff	P E S S O
7. _____ Norton	A E W D D R

DOWN

CLUE	ANSWER
1. Took place subsequently	N U E D E S
2. Bunched	D R O G P U E
3. Capital of Cyprus	A I S I O C N
4. Truly	E E N I D D

CLUE: This country has the highest per capita income of any country in southeast Asia.

BONUS ○○○○○○○○○

How to play — Complete the crossword puzzle by looking at the clues and unscrambling the answers. When the puzzle is complete, unscramble the circled letters to solve the bonus.

PUZZLE #119

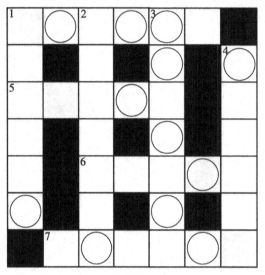

JUMBLE CROSSWORDS™

ACROSS

CLUE	ANSWER
1. Meal _____	T K E I T C
5. Change	N S O I C
6. Foolish	P T I E N
7. People	E N I B S G

DOWN

CLUE	ANSWER
1. Heart	T R C E I K
2. Food style	U N I S I E C
3. _____ time zone	A R N E S T E
4. Time periods	H N O M T S

BONUS

CLUE: The first _____ _____ was installed in Oklahoma City in 1935.

◯◯◯◯◯◯◯ ◯◯◯◯◯◯

How to play — Complete the crossword puzzle by looking at the clues and unscrambling the answers. When the puzzle is complete, unscramble the circled letters to solve the bonus.

#120

JUMBLE CROSSWORDS™

ACROSS

CLUE	ANSWER
1. Water _____	P U L P Y S
5. Firm fabric	N E D I M
6. _____ stew	R I H I S
7. Little _____	A E E G L U

DOWN

CLUE	ANSWER
1. Calm	D E S T A E
2. Contemplative	N E E P I S V
3. Small mammal	L G E I M N M
4. Long-running comic strip	R I A H C E

BONUS CLUE: The largest inland body of water on Earth.

How to play   Complete the crossword puzzle by looking at the clues and unscrambling the answers. When the puzzle is complete, unscramble the circled letters to solve the bonus.

#121

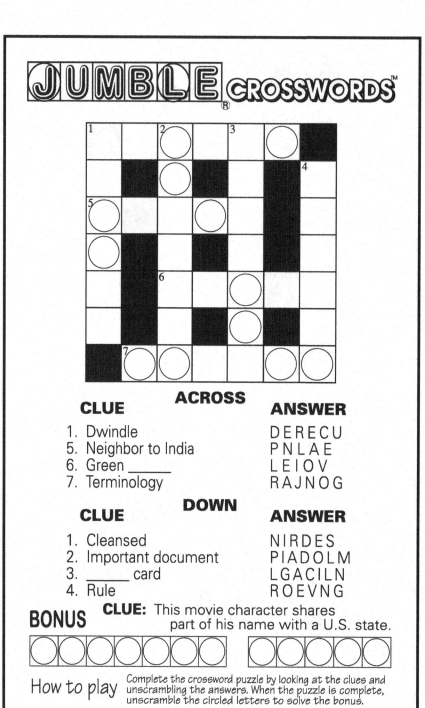

JUMBLE® CROSSWORDS™

ACROSS

CLUE	ANSWER
1. Dwindle	DERECU
5. Neighbor to India	PNLAE
6. Green _____	LEIOV
7. Terminology	RAJNOG

DOWN

CLUE	ANSWER
1. Cleansed	NIRDES
2. Important document	PIADOLM
3. _____ card	LGACILN
4. Rule	ROEVNG

BONUS **CLUE:** This movie character shares part of his name with a U.S. state.

How to play — Complete the crossword puzzle by looking at the clues and unscrambling the answers. When the puzzle is complete, unscramble the circled letters to solve the bonus.

JUMBLE CROSSWORDS™

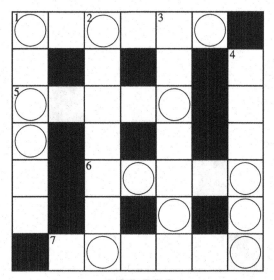

ACROSS

CLUE	ANSWER
1. _____ sale	RGGEAA
5. Type of home	LOIOG
6. Comment	PNTIU
7. _____ tree	HRYRCE

DOWN

CLUE	ANSWER
1. Steel _____	TUIRGA
2. North Carolina city	LARIEHG
3. Large fish	ROGPURE
4. Loose-lipped	ACYTHT

BONUS **CLUE:** This cartoon mascot debuted on boxes in the early fifties.

How to play Complete the crossword puzzle by looking at the clues and unscrambling the answers. When the puzzle is complete, unscramble the circled letters to solve the bonus.

P U Z Z L E

 #123

JUMBLE CROSSWORDS™

ACROSS

CLUE	ANSWER
1. Entrance	ROPLAT
5. Shrink away	ERWOC
6. One of 50	DHIAO
7. Cuts	SRVEES

DOWN

CLUE	ANSWER
1. Vacuum-_____	KADPCE
2. Revise	EERRTIW
3. Land	RACAEEG
4. Moves swiftly	TCOSOS

BONUS CLUE: There are more than 200 species of these.

How to play — Complete the crossword puzzle by looking at the clues and unscrambling the answers. When the puzzle is complete, unscramble the circled letters to solve the bonus.

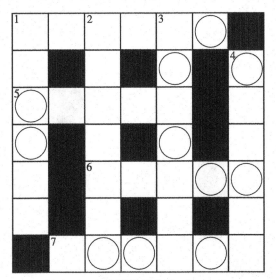

JUMBLE CROSSWORDS™

ACROSS

CLUE	ANSWER
1. Tongue's partner	GROEVO
5. Group	TBHCA
6. Happen	RCUCO
7. By this means	BREHYE

DOWN

CLUE	ANSWER
1. Mischievous sprite	BOGNIL
2. Aftermath	TOOCEMU
3. Motor _____	HEVCIEL
4. Turbulent	TYSROM

BONUS **CLUE:** Maine is a leading producer of these.

How to play Complete the crossword puzzle by looking at the clues and unscrambling the answers. When the puzzle is complete, unscramble the circled letters to solve the bonus.

#125

JUMBLE CROSSWORDS™

ACROSS

CLUE	ANSWER
1. Important commodity	ATSELP
5. Famous slugger	NROAA
6. Primitive	ENIAV
7. Combined	MGDREE

DOWN

CLUE	ANSWER
1. Panicked	ACSDER
2. Plan	RRGAAEN
3. Desire	NNGOILG
4. Story	EGLNDE

BONUS **CLUE:** Eisenhower renamed this after his grandson.

How to play Complete the crossword puzzle by looking at the clues and unscrambling the answers. When the puzzle is complete, unscramble the circled letters to solve the bonus.

PUZZLE

#126

JUMBLE® CROSSWORDS™

ACROSS

CLUE	ANSWER
1. Bull	WHGSAHO
5. Leader	LRURE
6. Yorba _____	NILAD
7. Least hasty	EOLSWTS

DOWN

CLUE	ANSWER
1. _____ racing	RSSHENA
2. Famous Italian	LOAGILE
3. Set up	RGARNEA
4. Fire _____	DYNHART

BONUS **CLUE:** This is 1,500 years older than the Roman Colosseum.

How to play Complete the crossword puzzle by looking at the clues and unscrambling the answers. When the puzzle is complete, unscramble the circled letters to solve the bonus.

PUZZLE

#127

JUMBLE CROSSWORDS™

ACROSS

CLUE		ANSWER
1.	Fleet	A A A D M R
5.	Phase	A C E F T
6.	Land formation	A L L O T
7.	License _____	A E L P S T

DOWN

CLUE		ANSWER
1.	Love _____	A A F F I R
2.	Kirk's son	A C E H I L M
3.	Home to Fisher Tower	D E I O R T T
4.	Horns	B E G L S U

BONUS

CLUE: Special arrangement

How to play Complete the crossword puzzle by looking at the clues and unscrambling the answers. When the puzzle is complete, unscramble the circled letters to solve the bonus.

#128

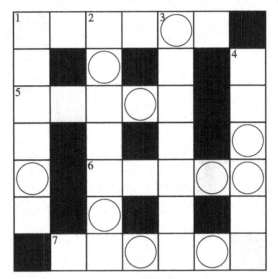

JUMBLE CROSSWORDS™

ACROSS

CLUE	ANSWER
1. Look over	E U S E P R
5. _____ point	A E R T X
6. Mountainous country	P L E A N
7. Frank	D I A C D N

DOWN

CLUE	ANSWER
1. Vow	P E E G L D
2. Round room	T O R N U A D
3. Overwhelmed	D W E S P A M
4. Questioned	L O P D E L

BONUS CLUE: This first appeared in the late 1700s.

How to play — Complete the crossword puzzle by looking at the clues and unscrambling the answers. When the puzzle is complete, unscramble the circled letters to solve the bonus.

JUMBLE CROSSWORDS™

ACROSS

CLUE	ANSWER
1. Stolen	B N D E B A
5. High-pitched sound	P E B E L
6. _____ Coast	R O Y I V
7. Disintegrated	T E M D E L

DOWN

CLUE	ANSWER
1. Not any person	B O N Y D O
2. Collective home	E I H E B E V
3. Utilize	P X E I O T L
4. Frolicked	A L P D E Y

BONUS   **CLUE:** G.W.'s note

◯◯◯ ◯◯◯◯◯◯◯ ◯◯◯◯◯

How to play   Complete the crossword puzzle by looking at the clues and unscrambling the answers. When the puzzle is complete, unscramble the circled letters to solve the bonus.

#130

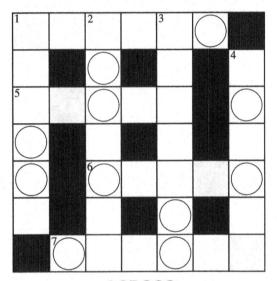

JUMBLE CROSSWORDS™

ACROSS

CLUE		ANSWER
1.	Petty	TLPYRA
5.	Occurs	NDSAW
6.	_____ Province	HENIR
7.	Home to Lake Vättern	DWNEES

DOWN

CLUE		ANSWER
1.	Watery collection	LUEPDD
2.	Person with little taste	RBWOLWO
3.	Repeal	DRNEICS
4.	Clay _____	PENIOG

BONUS CLUE: This is about twice the size of Manhattan.

How to play Complete the crossword puzzle by looking at the clues and unscrambling the answers. When the puzzle is complete, unscramble the circled letters to solve the bonus.

JUMBLE CROSSWORDS™

ACROSS

CLUE	ANSWER
1. Large force	ENGOIL
5. Fight	RWLBA
6. Double-_____	TIDIG
7. Giant _____	NAAPSD

DOWN

CLUE	ANSWER
1. Adhesive stamps	BALSLE
2. A female relative	ARGDNAM
3. Compelled	BGDEIOL
4. Sloping channels	UCSTEH

BONUS

CLUE: About 40 percent of adult women were once _____ _____.

○○○○ ○○○○○○

How to play — Complete the crossword puzzle by looking at the clues and unscrambling the answers. When the puzzle is complete, unscramble the circled letters to solve the bonus.

JUMBLE® CROSSWORDS™
Jackpot

ACROSS

CLUE	ANSWER
1. Bring into accord	N U A T E T
5. Large meal	T F E S A
6. Pattern	B H I A T
7. Mallets	L A S G E V

DOWN

CLUE	ANSWER
1. Influence	F E F C A T
2. Air tube	A R T H C A E
3. Renowned	T O N B A E L
4. Endings	D T E H S A

How to play: Complete the crossword puzzle by looking at the clues and unscrambling the answers. When the puzzle is complete, unscramble the circled letters to solve the bonuses.

CLUE: Happens when you're nervous.

DOUBLE BONUS

The circled letters can be unscrambled to form two different bonus answers.

CLUE: Talented

#133

JUMBLE CROSSWORDS™

ACROSS

CLUE	ANSWER
1. "I"	DINIEO
5. Mercury or January	FTRIS
6. You are one	ENIBG
7. Fuses	RMSEEG

DOWN

CLUE	ANSWER
1. Ingrain	NSEIUF
2. Strong	RDBLUEA
3. Zip	TNGIONH
4. Puts on	ASTESG

How to play: Complete the crossword puzzle by looking at the clues and unscrambling the answers. When the puzzle is complete, unscramble the circled letters to solve the bonuses.

DOUBLE BONUS

The circled letters can be unscrambled to form two different bonus answers.

CLUE: Malice

CLUE: Harsh

#134

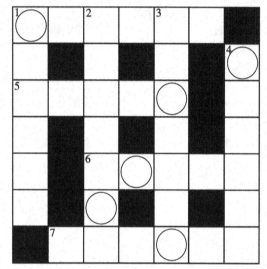

ACROSS

CLUE	ANSWER
1. Compassionate	DTNREE
5. Smarted	NSTGU
6. Respond	ATCER
7. Moves smoothly	DLSSIE

DOWN

CLUE	ANSWER
1. Proven	ETDETS
2. Dispassionate	UETNLAR
3. New _____	NGEALDN
4. Free	ARGIST

How to play: Complete the crossword puzzle by looking at the clues and unscrambling the answers. When the puzzle is complete, unscramble the circled letters to solve the bonuses.

CLUE: Device

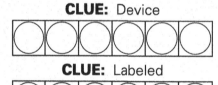

DOUBLE BONUS

The circled letters can be unscrambled to form two different bonus answers.

CLUE: Labeled

#135

JUMBLE CROSSWORDS™

ACROSS

CLUE	ANSWER
1. Award-winning movie	N G A I H D
5. Muffles	M S T U E
6. Increase	A S R I E
7. Though	T L I E A B

DOWN

CLUE	ANSWER
1. Maneuver	T G I M A B
2. Innate	A N R U L A T
3. Contrary	E H O I S T L
4. What some bugs do	F I T N E S

How to play: Complete the crossword puzzle by looking at the clues and unscrambling the answers. When the puzzle is complete, unscramble the circled letters to solve the bonuses.

CLUE: Through

CLUE: Diabolical

DOUBLE BONUS

The circled letters can be unscrambled to form two different bonus answers.

JUMBLE® CROSSWORDS™

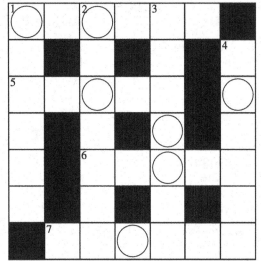

ACROSS

CLUE	ANSWER
1. Front _____	B E M P R U
5. Musical Italian	D I E R V
6. Relative	E I N C E
7. _____ pine	T O S H C C

DOWN

CLUE	ANSWER
1. A buffalo, for example	E I B N O V
2. Stupid	R I M C N O O
3. Clear	T N I E E D V
4. _____ Stalin	P E J O H S

How to play: Complete the crossword puzzle by looking at the clues and unscrambling the answers. When the puzzle is complete, unscramble the circled letters to solve the bonuses.

DOUBLE BONUS

The circled letters can be unscrambled to form two different bonus answers.

CLUE: Extra _____

○○○○○○○

CLUE: Reason to yawn

○○○○○○○

#137

JUMBLE CROSSWORDS™

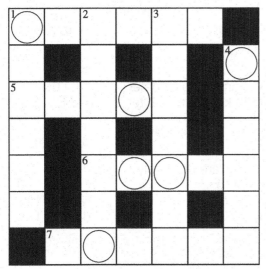

ACROSS

CLUE	ANSWER
1. _____ music	P G S O L E
5. Short notice	R B B L U
6. Zealot	E I F D N
7. Count	N U C E S S

DOWN

CLUE	ANSWER
1. Tailless ape	N I G O B B
2. Jumble	H F U S E L F
3. Symbols	B M E E L S M
4. Directors	U S E D I G

How to play: Complete the crossword puzzle by looking at the clues and unscrambling the answers. When the puzzle is complete, unscramble the circled letters to solve the bonuses.

DOUBLE BONUS

The circled letters can be unscrambled to form two different bonus answers.

CLUE: Miller or Jackson

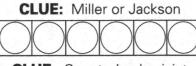

CLUE: Counter's physicist

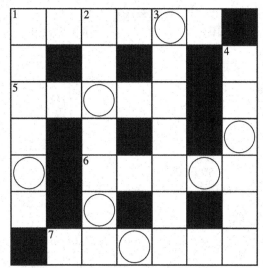

ACROSS

CLUE	ANSWER
1. Fall	TUNAMU
5. African region	NDSAU
6. Springtime bloomer	LLICA
7. Kirk's control center	DREIBG

DOWN

CLUE	ANSWER
1. Declare positively	TSREAS
2. Child	LDEDROT
3. Mixed	NDGIMEL
4. Full _____	RICELC

How to play: Complete the crossword puzzle by looking at the clues and unscrambling the answers. When the puzzle is complete, unscramble the circled letters to solve the bonuses.

DOUBLE BONUS
The circled letters can be unscrambled to form two different bonus answers.

CLUE: Secret _____

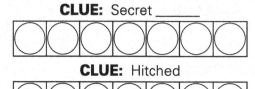

CLUE: Hitched

PUZZLE #139

JUMBLE CROSSWORDS™

ACROSS

CLUE	ANSWER
1. Indulge	MAPREP
5. _____ Lauren	LARHP
6. Infuse	BMIEU
7. Section	ERCOTS

DOWN

CLUE	ANSWER
1. Unit of measure	RACESP
2. Debilitating feeling	LAMIAES
3. Show	HIXIEBT
4. Make beloved	DENRAE

How to play: Complete the crossword puzzle by looking at the clues and unscrambling the answers. When the puzzle is complete, unscramble the circled letters to solve the bonuses.

CLUE: Counselors

CLUE: _____ truck

DOUBLE BONUS
The circled letters can be unscrambled to form two different bonus answers.

PUZZLE #140

JUMBLE CROSSWORDS™

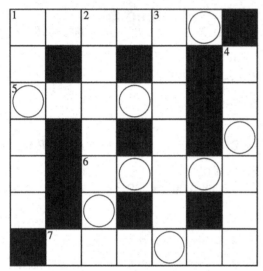

ACROSS

CLUE	ANSWER
1. Breath in	LHIAEN
5. Mature	NPEIR
6. Foil	AEVED
7. Trees	PSANES

DOWN

CLUE	ANSWER
1. Middle Eastern country	RISALE
2. Unlucky	LPAHSSE
3. Connection	NILAKEG
4. Coercion	ERSUSD

How to play: Complete the crossword puzzle by looking at the clues and unscrambling the answers. When the puzzle is complete, unscramble the circled letters to solve the bonuses.

DOUBLE BONUS

The circled letters can be unscrambled to form two different bonus answers.

CLUE: Annulled

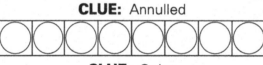

CLUE: Quiet

PUZZLE

#141

JUMBLE CROSSWORDS™

ACROSS

CLUE	ANSWER
1. Common _____	NUORDG
5. _____ Cushing	TPREE
6. Coarse	HUGOR
7. Secret	EVROTC

DOWN

CLUE	ANSWER
1. Burrowing animal	PRHOEG
2. Home to Thunder Bay	TINORAO
3. Foster	RUNUTER
4. Outcome	HTUOSP

How to play: Complete the crossword puzzle by looking at the clues and unscrambling the answers. When the puzzle is complete, unscramble the circled letters to solve the bonuses.

DOUBLE BONUS

The circled letters can be unscrambled to form two different bonus answers.

CLUE: Repairing

CLUE: Type of baseball game

143

PUZZLE #142

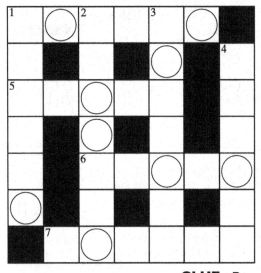

ACROSS

CLUE	ANSWER
1. Foil	HTWTRA
5. With	NOMGA
6. Tact	PESIO
7. EU Member	ERGCEE

DOWN

CLUE	ANSWER
1. Tracked	ARTDEC
2. Lie	HORWPEP
3. _____ band	TGIAMRE
4. Hinder	PDEIEM

How to play: Complete the crossword puzzle by looking at the clues and unscrambling the answers. When the puzzle is complete, unscramble the circled letters to solve the bonuses.

DOUBLE BONUS

The circled letters can be unscrambled to form two different bonus answers.

CLUE: Beautiful goddess

CLUE: Decreased in size, degenerated

#143

JUMBLE CROSSWORDS™

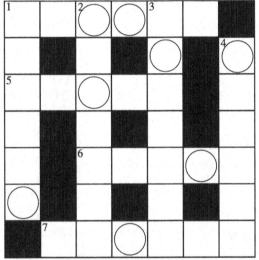

ACROSS

CLUE	ANSWER
1. Special _____	RETROP
5. Dental _____	LSOSF
6. Fibbing	YGNIL
7. A sixth	ARDIYF

DOWN

CLUE	ANSWER
1. Tax _____	FERDNU
2. Reason to call 911	RPLWROE
3. Cancel	ENDRICS
4. Unkempt	AHSYGG

How to play: Complete the crossword puzzle by looking at the clues and unscrambling the answers. When the puzzle is complete, unscramble the circled letters to solve the bonuses.

DOUBLE BONUS

The circled letters can be unscrambled to form two different bonus answers.

CLUE: Corrupted

CLUE: A Greek god

JUMBLE CROSSWORDS™

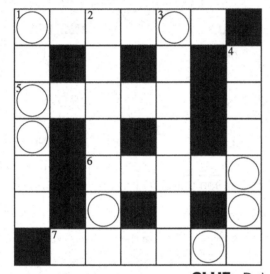

ACROSS

CLUE	ANSWER
1. Decrease	DREECU
5. Store	PTOED
6. Dodge	EDEAV
7. Exercise	NLOSES

DOWN

CLUE	ANSWER
1. Pungent root	DRHISA
2. Drain	EEEPDLT
3. Small sword	UTSCALS
4. Rule	NOGEVR

How to play: Complete the crossword puzzle by looking at the clues and unscrambling the answers. When the puzzle is complete, unscramble the circled letters to solve the bonuses.

CLUE: Debtor's obverse

DOUBLE BONUS

The circled letters can be unscrambled to form two different bonus answers.

CLUE: Funeral _____

JUMBLE® CROSSWORDS™ Jackpot

TRIPLE BONUS

PUZZLES

JUMBLE CROSSWORDS™

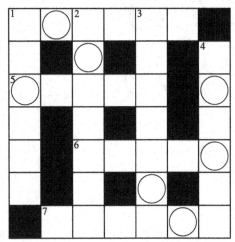

ACROSS

CLUE	ANSWER
1. Counsel	D V E I A S
5. _____ sauce	T A S A P
6. False	U G O S B
7. Prosperous time	A Y H D Y E

DOWN

CLUE	ANSWER
1. Angle	P S A T C E
2. Seen	L I E I B S V
3. Caught	N G S D G A E
4. Secure	U T Y T S R

How to play: Complete the crossword puzzle by looking at the clues and unscrambling the answers. When the puzzle is complete, unscramble the circled letters to solve the bonuses.

TRIPLE BONUS
The circled letters can be unscrambled to form three different bonus answers.

CLUE: Disposable _____

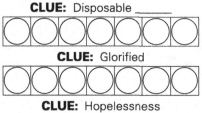

CLUE: Glorified

CLUE: Hopelessness

PUZZLE
#146

JUMBLE CROSSWORDS™

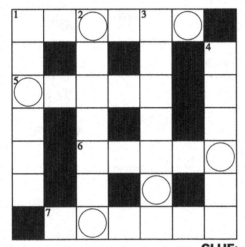

ACROSS
CLUE — **ANSWER**

1. Compress — RSHKIN
5. With — NMOAG
6. _____ pole — ETTMO
7. Deep-seated feeling — UGGDRE

DOWN
CLUE — **ANSWER**

1. Contained — AESDEL
2. _____ tail — SOORRET
3. Nullified — TAGEEDN
4. Stand in the way of — ESITMY

How to play: Complete the crossword puzzle by looking at the clues and unscrambling the answers. When the puzzle is complete, unscramble the circled letters to solve the bonuses.

TRIPLE BONUS
The circled letters can be unscrambled to form three different bonus answers.

CLUE: Indicator
○○○○○○

CLUE: Comment
○○○○○○

CLUE: Popular TV neighbor
○○○○○○

JUMBLE CROSSWORDS™

ACROSS

CLUE	ANSWER
1. _____ table	N R I D E N
5. Wharton or Nesbit	T D I E H
6. Moon motion	B R O I T
7. Flower part	L I P I T S

DOWN

CLUE	ANSWER
1. Dismal	R E D Y A R
2. Home to about 2 million	N R I A O I B
3. Show	H I X E I B T
4. Group	A L E C T R

How to play: Complete the crossword puzzle by looking at the clues and unscrambling the answers. When the puzzle is complete, unscramble the circled letters to solve the bonuses.

TRIPLE BONUS

The circled letters can be unscrambled to form three different bonus answers.

CLUE: Stern or Boone

◯◯◯◯◯◯

CLUE: Self-_____

◯◯◯◯◯◯

CLUE: Caught, exposed

◯◯◯◯◯◯

#148

ACROSS

CLUE	ANSWER
1. Mixture	T P N O I O
5. Egg partner	N A B O C
6. Story	B A F E L
7. Shut	L E S O D C

DOWN

CLUE	ANSWER
1. Out in the open	B C I L U P
2. Doesn't give offense	T T C A L U F
3. Anthology	N M B I S U O
4. Actually	D I E N D E

How to play: Complete the crossword puzzle by looking at the clues and unscrambling the answers. When the puzzle is complete, unscramble the circled letters to solve the bonuses.

TRIPLE
BONUS

The circled letters can be unscrambled to form three different bonus answers.

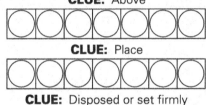

CLUE: Above

CLUE: Place

CLUE: Disposed or set firmly

#149

JUMBLE CROSSWORDS™

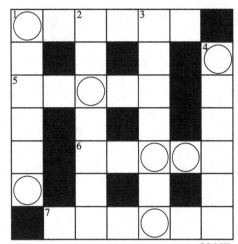

ACROSS

CLUE	ANSWER
1. Most current	TALETS
5. Pine _____, Arkansas	UFLFB
6. Brownie _____	NOIPT
7. _____ fracture	RTSSSE

DOWN

CLUE	ANSWER
1. Tossed	BOLDEB
2. Proclaim	RTUPTEM
3. Do	FUSIFEC
4. Cooking frames	ERSGAT

How to play: Complete the crossword puzzle by looking at the clues and unscrambling the answers. When the puzzle is complete, unscramble the circled letters to solve the bonuses.

TRIPLE BONUS

The circled letters can be unscrambled to form three different bonus answers.

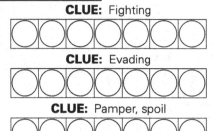

CLUE: Fighting

CLUE: Evading

CLUE: Pamper, spoil

#150

JUMBLE CROSSWORDS™

ACROSS

CLUE	ANSWER
1. Neighbor to Zambia	N G A A L O
5. Foundation	A I B S S
6. Association	N N I O U
7. Atomic _____	E T H I W G

DOWN

CLUE	ANSWER
1. Photo _____	B L A S M U
2. Expressive movement	E E S G U T R
3. Durable	T I A L G S N
4. _____ school	A E G N T M

How to play: Complete the crossword puzzle by looking at the clues and unscrambling the answers. When the puzzle is complete, unscramble the circled letters to solve the bonuses.

TRIPLE BONUS

The circled letters can be unscrambled to form three different bonus answers.

CLUE: Type of alien

CLUE: Famous tennis player's first name

CLUE: Type of monkey

JUMBLE CROSSWORDS™

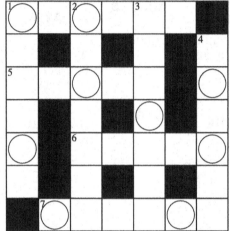

ACROSS

CLUE	ANSWER
1. Obedient	D E L O I C
5. Vertical	M L U B P
6. Southern key	R G A O L
7. Attack	L S A S I A

DOWN

CLUE	ANSWER
1. Rely	P D N E E D
2. Pairs	U O E S L P C
3. Sierra Leone's neighbor	B I L R I E A
4. Walk	R T S L L O

TRIPLE BONUS

The circled letters can be unscrambled to form three different bonus answers.

CLUE: Sold; _____ off

CLUE: Warned

CLUE: Higher _____

How to play: Complete the crossword puzzle by looking at the clues and unscrambling the answers. When the puzzle is complete, unscramble the circled letters to solve the bonuses.

#152

JUMBLE CROSSWORDS™

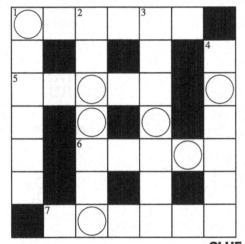

ACROSS

CLUE	ANSWER
1. Mystery	N M A E I G
5. Time and again	T F O N E
6. Facade	U E I G S
7. Home to the Garonne	F C A N R E

DOWN

CLUE	ANSWER
1. Unfold, mature	E E L V O V
2. 1, for example	T E E G I R N
3. Say	N M O E T I N
4. Shirt part	L V S E E E

How to play: Complete the crossword puzzle by looking at the clues and unscrambling the answers. When the puzzle is complete, unscramble the circled letters to solve the bonuses.

TRIPLE BONUS
The circled letters can be unscrambled to form three different bonus answers.

CLUE: A, B, C

CLUE: Colonizer

CLUE: Support frame

#153

JUMBLE CROSSWORDS™

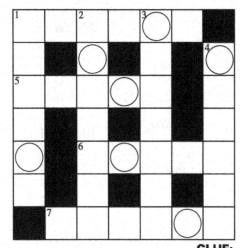

ACROSS

CLUE		ANSWER
1. Unshaken		TAYESD
5. Water _____		EIPPS
6. Increase		REIAS
7. Source		NGIOIR

DOWN

CLUE		ANSWER
1. Give		YULSPP
2. Hirohito		PRMREEO
3. Hurrying		HSNIGDA
4. Natural chamber		VAECNR

How to play: Complete the crossword puzzle by looking at the clues and unscrambling the answers. When the puzzle is complete, unscramble the circled letters to solve the bonuses.

CLUE: Asserted

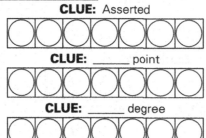

TRIPLE
BONUS

The circled letters can be unscrambled to form three different bonus answers.

CLUE: _____ point

CLUE: _____ degree

JUMBLE® CROSSWORDS™ Jackpot

JUMBLE® CROSSWORDS™

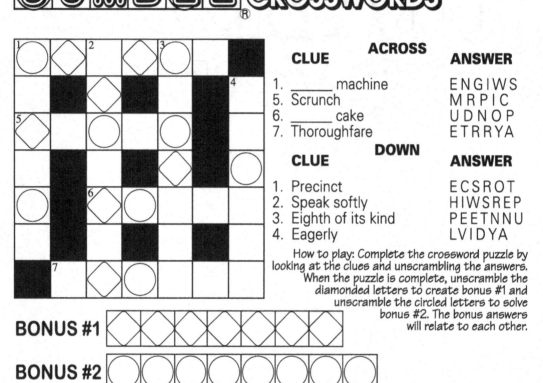

CLUE	ACROSS	ANSWER
1. _____ machine		E N G I W S
5. Scrunch		M R P I C
6. _____ cake		U D N O P
7. Thoroughfare		E T R R Y A

CLUE	DOWN	ANSWER
1. Precinct		E C S R O T
2. Speak softly		H I W S R E P
3. Eighth of its kind		P E E T N N U
4. Eagerly		L V I D Y A

How to play: Complete the crossword puzzle by looking at the clues and unscrambling the answers. When the puzzle is complete, unscramble the diamonded letters to create bonus #1 and unscramble the circled letters to solve bonus #2. The bonus answers will relate to each other.

BONUS #1

BONUS #2

#155

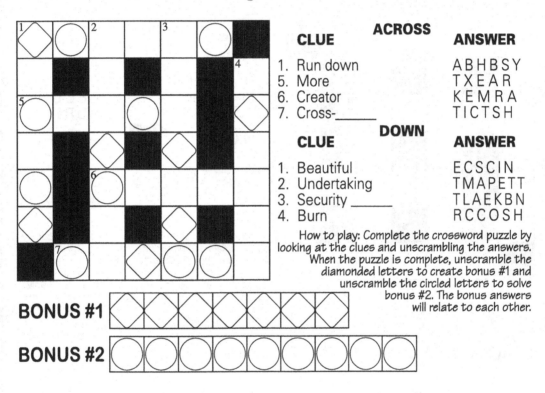

JUMBLE CROSSWORDS™

ACROSS

CLUE	ANSWER
1. Run down	A B H B S Y
5. More	T X E A R
6. Creator	K E M R A
7. Cross-_____	T I C T S H

DOWN

CLUE	ANSWER
1. Beautiful	E C S C I N
2. Undertaking	T M A P E T T
3. Security _____	T L A E K B N
4. Burn	R C C O S H

How to play: Complete the crossword puzzle by looking at the clues and unscrambling the answers. When the puzzle is complete, unscramble the diamonded letters to create bonus #1 and unscramble the circled letters to solve bonus #2. The bonus answers will relate to each other.

BONUS #1

BONUS #2

#156

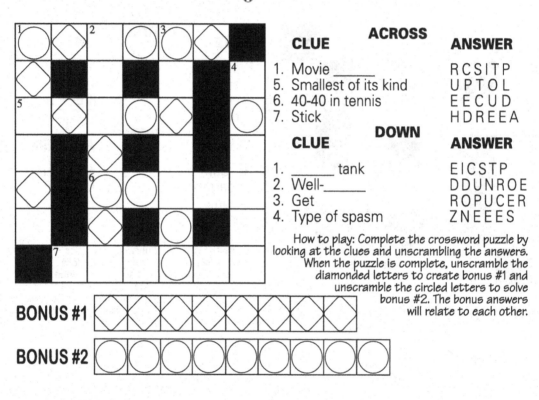

JUMBLE CROSSWORDS™

ACROSS

CLUE	ANSWER
1. Movie _____	RCSITP
5. Smallest of its kind	UPTOL
6. 40-40 in tennis	EECUD
7. Stick	HDREEA

DOWN

CLUE	ANSWER
1. _____ tank	EICSTP
2. Well-_____	DDUNROE
3. Get	ROPUCER
4. Type of spasm	ZNEEES

How to play: Complete the crossword puzzle by looking at the clues and unscrambling the answers. When the puzzle is complete, unscramble the diamonded letters to create bonus #1 and unscramble the circled letters to solve bonus #2. The bonus answers will relate to each other.

BONUS #1

BONUS #2

#157

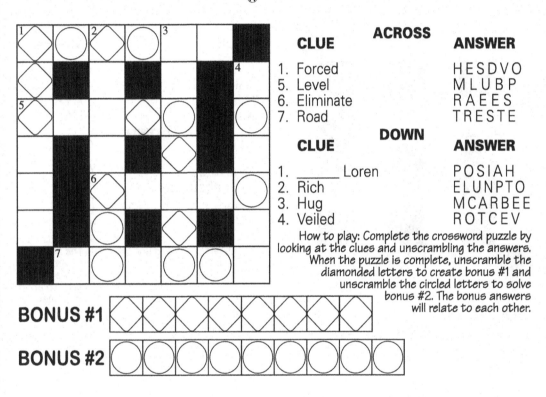

JUMBLE CROSSWORDS™

ACROSS

CLUE	ANSWER
1. Forced	HESDVO
5. Level	MLUBP
6. Eliminate	RAEES
7. Road	TRESTE

DOWN

CLUE	ANSWER
1. _____ Loren	POSIAH
2. Rich	ELUNPTO
3. Hug	MCARBEE
4. Veiled	ROTCEV

How to play: Complete the crossword puzzle by looking at the clues and unscrambling the answers. When the puzzle is complete, unscramble the diamonded letters to create bonus #1 and unscramble the circled letters to solve bonus #2. The bonus answers will relate to each other.

BONUS #1

BONUS #2

PUZZLE #158

JUMBLE CROSSWORDS™

ACROSS

CLUE	ANSWER
1. Overwhelm	NFELUG
5. Halley's claim to fame	MTEOC
6. Dead _____	HADAE
7. Stuck around	ETYDSA

DOWN

CLUE	ANSWER
1. Motivate	XEICET
2. Type of athlete	MGANYTS
3. State _____	TOLETYR
4. Long-_____	DNEIDW

How to play: Complete the crossword puzzle by looking at the clues and unscrambling the answers. When the puzzle is complete, unscramble the diamonded letters to create bonus #1 and unscramble the circled letters to solve bonus #2. The bonus answers will relate to each other.

BONUS #1

BONUS #2

#159

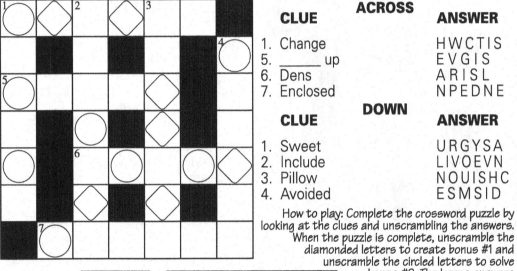

JUMBLE® CROSSWORDS™

ACROSS

CLUE	ANSWER
1. Change	HWCTIS
5. _____ up	EVGIS
6. Dens	ARISL
7. Enclosed	NPEDNE

DOWN

CLUE	ANSWER
1. Sweet	URGYSA
2. Include	LIVOEVN
3. Pillow	NOUISHC
4. Avoided	ESMSID

How to play: Complete the crossword puzzle by looking at the clues and unscrambling the answers. When the puzzle is complete, unscramble the diamonded letters to create bonus #1 and unscramble the circled letters to solve bonus #2. The bonus answers will relate to each other.

BONUS #1

BONUS #2

PUZZLE #160

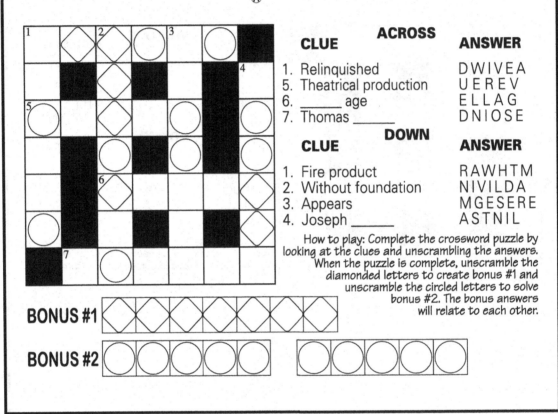

JUMBLE CROSSWORDS™

ACROSS

CLUE		ANSWER
1.	Relinquished	DWIVEA
5.	Theatrical production	UEREV
6.	_____ age	ELLAG
7.	Thomas _____	DNIOSE

DOWN

CLUE		ANSWER
1.	Fire product	RAWHTM
2.	Without foundation	NIVILDA
3.	Appears	MGESERE
4.	Joseph _____	ASTNIL

How to play: Complete the crossword puzzle by looking at the clues and unscrambling the answers. When the puzzle is complete, unscramble the diamonded letters to create bonus #1 and unscramble the circled letters to solve bonus #2. The bonus answers will relate to each other.

BONUS #1

BONUS #2

JUMBLE CROSSWORDS™

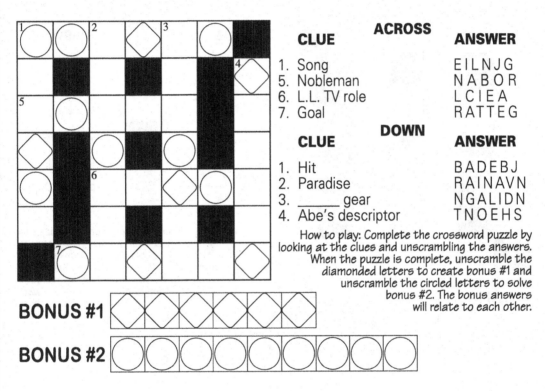

ACROSS

CLUE	ANSWER
1. Song	E I L N J G
5. Nobleman	N A B O R
6. L.L. TV role	L C I E A
7. Goal	R A T T E G

DOWN

CLUE	ANSWER
1. Hit	B A D E B J
2. Paradise	R A I N A V N
3. _____ gear	N G A L I D N
4. Abe's descriptor	T N O E H S

How to play: Complete the crossword puzzle by looking at the clues and unscrambling the answers. When the puzzle is complete, unscramble the diamonded letters to create bonus #1 and unscramble the circled letters to solve bonus #2. The bonus answers will relate to each other.

BONUS #1

BONUS #2

PUZZLE #162

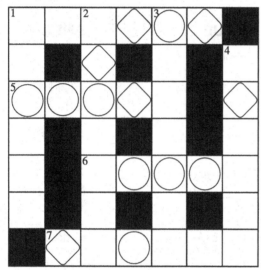

JUMBLE CROSSWORDS™

ACROSS

CLUE	ANSWER
1. Assumption	H E T R Y O
5. Angel _____	L F L A S
6. Oil _____	A P I T N
7. Eliminate	E E E L D T

DOWN

CLUE	ANSWER
1. Type of candy	E F O T E F
2. Total _____	L C E P I E S
3. Break	P E R E T I S
4. Move rapidly	R U H E L T

How to play: Complete the crossword puzzle by looking at the clues and unscrambling the answers. When the puzzle is complete, unscramble the diamonded letters to create bonus #1 and unscramble the circled letters to solve bonus #2. The bonus answers will relate to each other.

BONUS #1

BONUS #2

#163

JUMBLE CROSSWORDS™

ACROSS

CLUE	ANSWER
1. Harmful animals	M I R E V N
5. Eighth _____	T N S E O
6. Camel relative	M A A L L
7. _____ Ocean	C R A C I T

DOWN

CLUE	ANSWER
1. Destroyer	N A D V L A
2. American pit viper	R T A T R E L
3. Point in time	T N N T A I S
4. Picture of pieces	M C I S O A

How to play: Complete the crossword puzzle by looking at the clues and unscrambling the answers. When the puzzle is complete, unscramble the diamonded letters to create bonus #1 and unscramble the circled letters to solve bonus #2. The bonus answers will relate to each other.

BONUS #1

BONUS #2

JUMBLE CROSSWORDS™

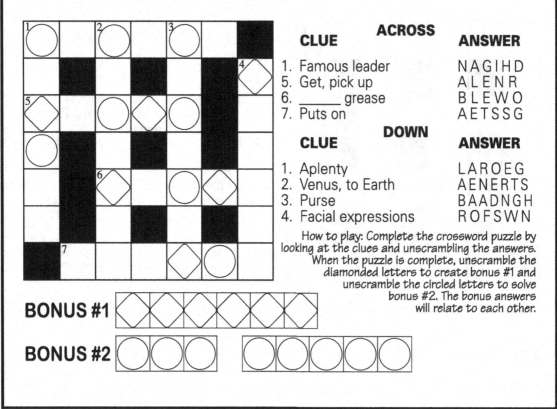

ACROSS

CLUE	ANSWER
1. Famous leader	NAGIHD
5. Get, pick up	ALENR
6. _____ grease	BLEWO
7. Puts on	AETSSG

DOWN

CLUE	ANSWER
1. Aplenty	LAROEG
2. Venus, to Earth	AENERTS
3. Purse	BAADNGH
4. Facial expressions	ROFSWN

How to play: Complete the crossword puzzle by looking at the clues and unscrambling the answers. When the puzzle is complete, unscramble the diamonded letters to create bonus #1 and unscramble the circled letters to solve bonus #2. The bonus answers will relate to each other.

BONUS #1

BONUS #2

PUZZLE #165

JUMBLE CROSSWORDS™

ACROSS

CLUE		ANSWER
1. Igneous rock		A S B T L A
5. Savory smell		M O A A R
6. Broods		L U S S K
7. Small "+"		T O R O P N

DOWN

CLUE		ANSWER
1. Short-legged mammal		B L G A E E
2. Supporter		O P S S N R O
3. Flier		T A E L L E F
4. _____ River		U O S D H N

How to play: Complete the crossword puzzle by looking at the clues and unscrambling the answers. When the puzzle is complete, unscramble the diamonded letters to create bonus #1 and unscramble the circled letters to solve bonus #2. The bonus answers will relate to each other.

BONUS #1

BONUS #2

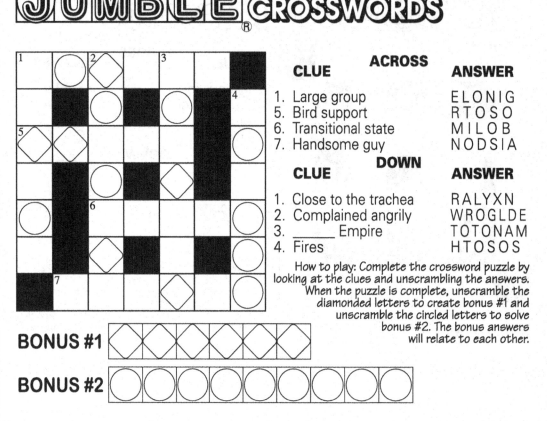

JUMBLE CROSSWORDS™

ACROSS

CLUE	ANSWER
1. Large group	ELONIG
5. Bird support	RTOSO
6. Transitional state	MILOB
7. Handsome guy	NODSIA

DOWN

CLUE	ANSWER
1. Close to the trachea	RALYXN
2. Complained angrily	WROGLDE
3. _____ Empire	TOTONAM
4. Fires	HTOSOS

How to play: Complete the crossword puzzle by looking at the clues and unscrambling the answers. When the puzzle is complete, unscramble the diamonded letters to create bonus #1 and unscramble the circled letters to solve bonus #2. The bonus answers will relate to each other.

BONUS #1

BONUS #2

JUMBLE® CROSSWORDS™ Jackpot

PUZZLE #167

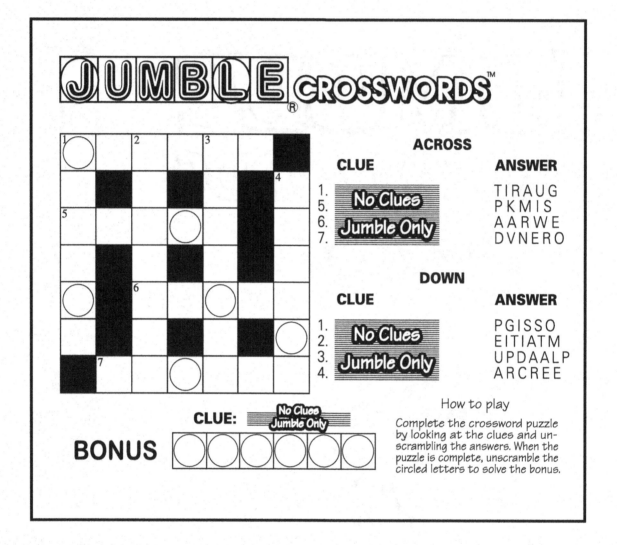

JUMBLE® CROSSWORDS™

ACROSS

	CLUE	ANSWER
1.		TIRAUG
5.	No Clues	PKMIS
6.	Jumble Only	AARWE
7.		DVNERO

DOWN

	CLUE	ANSWER
1.		PGISSO
2.	No Clues	EITIATM
3.	Jumble Only	UPDAALP
4.		ARCREE

How to play

Complete the crossword puzzle by looking at the clues and unscrambling the answers. When the puzzle is complete, unscramble the circled letters to solve the bonus.

CLUE: No Clues Jumble Only

BONUS

172

#168

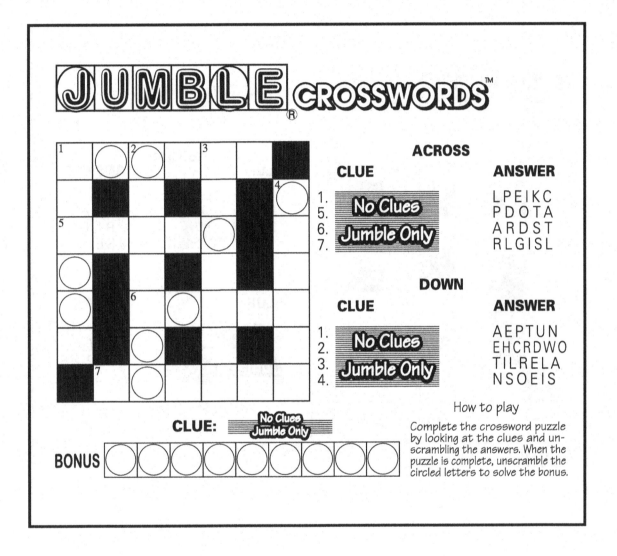

JUMBLE® CROSSWORDS™

ACROSS

CLUE	ANSWER
1.	LPEIKC
5. No Clues	PDOTA
6. Jumble Only	ARDST
7.	RLGISL

DOWN

CLUE	ANSWER
1.	AEPTUN
2. No Clues	EHCRDWO
3. Jumble Only	TILRELA
4.	NSOEIS

How to play

Complete the crossword puzzle by looking at the clues and unscrambling the answers. When the puzzle is complete, unscramble the circled letters to solve the bonus.

CLUE: No Clues Jumble Only

BONUS ◯◯◯◯◯◯◯◯◯

JUMBLE® CROSSWORDS™

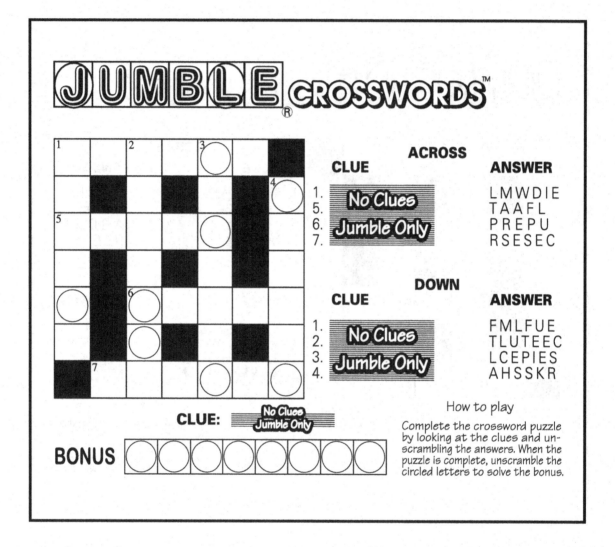

ACROSS

CLUE	ANSWER
1. No Clues	LMWDIE
5.	TAAFL
6. Jumble Only	PREPU
7.	RSESEC

DOWN

CLUE	ANSWER
1. No Clues	FMLFUE
2.	TLUTEEC
3. Jumble Only	LCEPIES
4.	AHSSKR

How to play

Complete the crossword puzzle by looking at the clues and un-scrambling the answers. When the puzzle is complete, unscramble the circled letters to solve the bonus.

CLUE: No Clues Jumble Only

BONUS

PUZZLE

#170

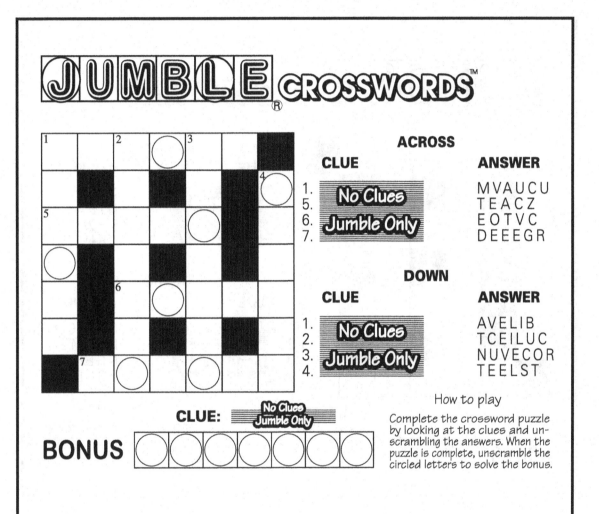

JUMBLE® CROSSWORDS™

ACROSS

CLUE	ANSWER
1.	MVAUCU
5. No Clues	TEACZ
6. Jumble Only	EOTVC
7.	DEEEGR

DOWN

CLUE	ANSWER
1.	AVELIB
2. No Clues	TCEILUC
3. Jumble Only	NUVECOR
4.	TEELST

How to play

Complete the crossword puzzle by looking at the clues and unscrambling the answers. When the puzzle is complete, unscramble the circled letters to solve the bonus.

CLUE: No Clues Jumble Only

BONUS ◯◯◯◯◯◯◯

 #171

JUMBLE® CROSSWORDS™

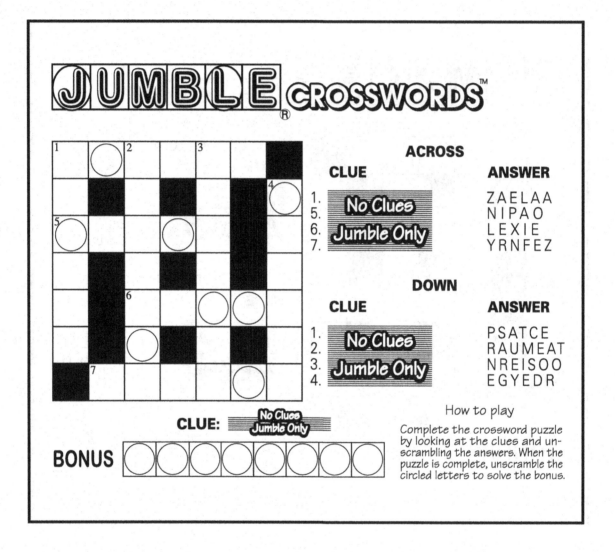

ACROSS

CLUE	ANSWER
1. No Clues	ZAELAA
5.	NIPAO
6. Jumble Only	LEXIE
7.	YRNFEZ

DOWN

CLUE	ANSWER
1. No Clues	PSATCE
2.	RAUMEAT
3. Jumble Only	NREISOO
4.	EGYEDR

How to play

Complete the crossword puzzle by looking at the clues and unscrambling the answers. When the puzzle is complete, unscramble the circled letters to solve the bonus.

CLUE: No Clues Jumble Only

BONUS ○○○○○○○○

#172

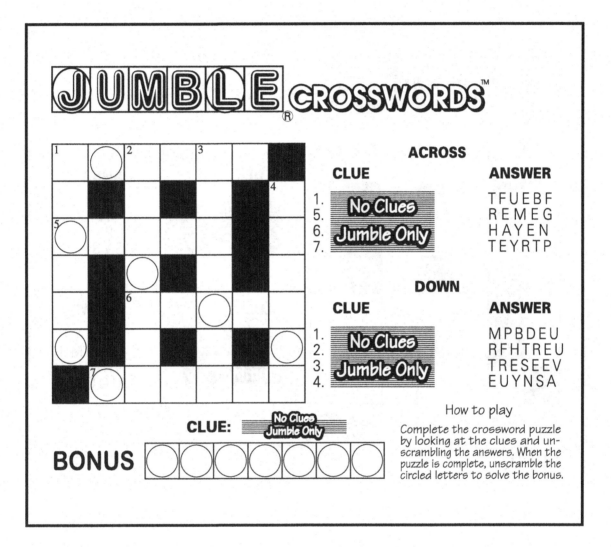

JUMBLE® CROSSWORDS™

ACROSS

CLUE	ANSWER
1. No Clues	TFUEBF
5.	REMEG
6. Jumble Only	HAYEN
7.	TEYRTP

DOWN

CLUE	ANSWER
1. No Clues	MPBDEU
2.	RFHTREU
3. Jumble Only	TRESEEV
4.	EUYNSA

How to play

Complete the crossword puzzle by looking at the clues and un-scrambling the answers. When the puzzle is complete, unscramble the circled letters to solve the bonus.

CLUE: No Clues Jumble Only

BONUS ○○○○○○○

#173

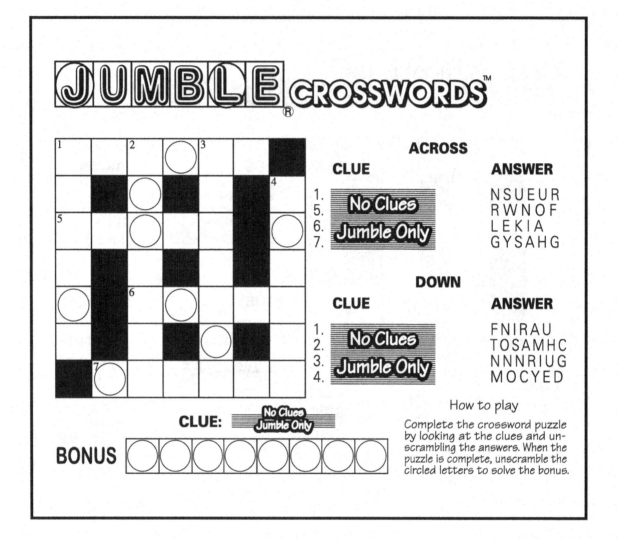

JUMBLE CROSSWORDS™

ACROSS

CLUE	ANSWER
1.	NSUEUR
5. No Clues	RWNOF
6. Jumble Only	LEKIA
7.	GYSAHG

DOWN

CLUE	ANSWER
1.	FNIRAU
2. No Clues	TOSAMHC
3. Jumble Only	NNNRIUG
4.	MOCYED

How to play

Complete the crossword puzzle by looking at the clues and un-scrambling the answers. When the puzzle is complete, unscramble the circled letters to solve the bonus.

CLUE: No Clues Jumble Only

BONUS

PUZZLE

#174

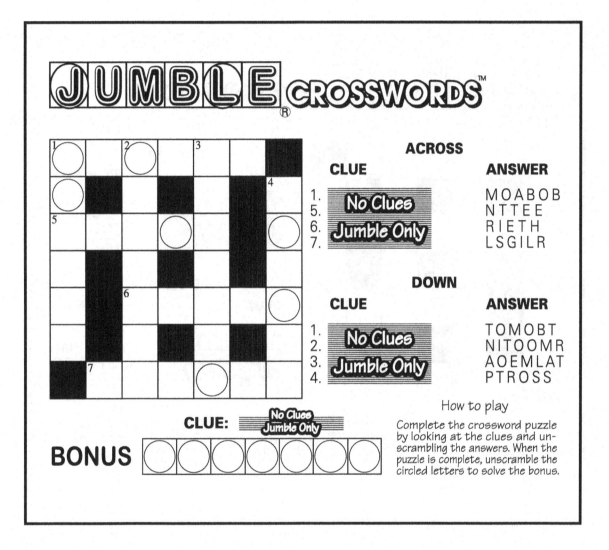

JUMBLE® CROSSWORDS™

ACROSS

CLUE		ANSWER
1.	No Clues	MOABOB
5.		NTTEE
6.	Jumble Only	RIETH
7.		LSGILR

DOWN

CLUE		ANSWER
1.	No Clues	TOMOBT
2.		NITOOMR
3.	Jumble Only	AOEMLAT
4.		PTROSS

How to play

Complete the crossword puzzle by looking at the clues and unscrambling the answers. When the puzzle is complete, unscramble the circled letters to solve the bonus.

CLUE: No Clues / Jumble Only

BONUS ○○○○○○○

#175

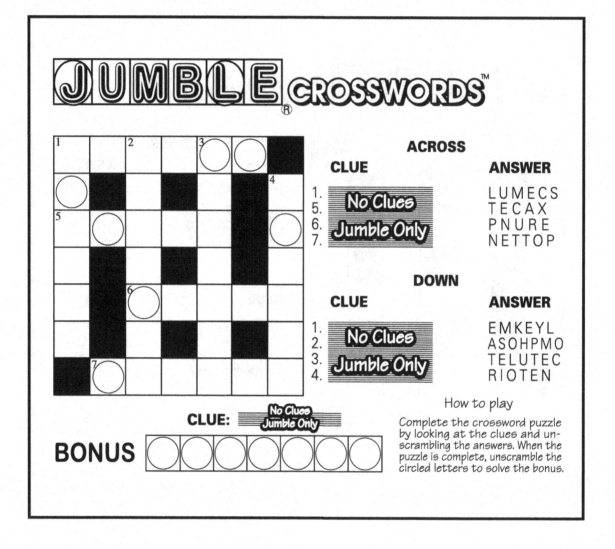

JUMBLE CROSSWORDS™

ACROSS

	CLUE	ANSWER
1.	No Clues	LUMECS
5.		TECAX
6.	Jumble Only	PNURE
7.		NETTOP

DOWN

	CLUE	ANSWER
1.	No Clues	EMKEYL
2.		ASOHPMO
3.	Jumble Only	TELUTEC
4.		RIOTEN

How to play

Complete the crossword puzzle by looking at the clues and unscrambling the answers. When the puzzle is complete, unscramble the circled letters to solve the bonus.

CLUE: No Clues Jumble Only

BONUS ○○○○○○○

PUZZLE
#176

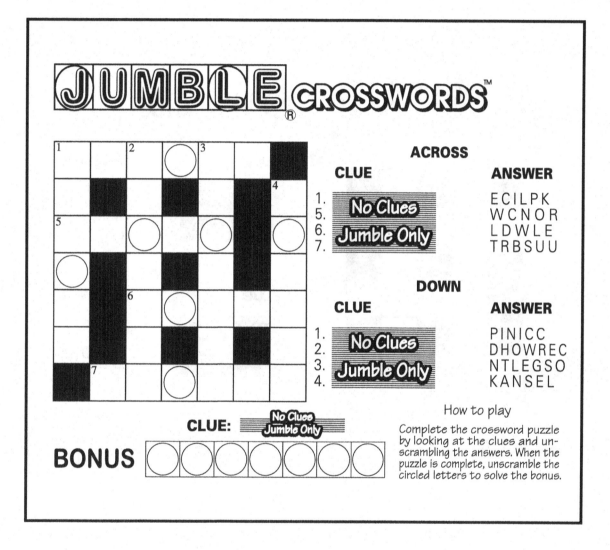

JUMBLE CROSSWORDS™

ACROSS

CLUE		ANSWER
1.		ECILPK
5.	No Clues	WCNOR
6.	Jumble Only	LDWLE
7.		TRBSUU

DOWN

CLUE		ANSWER
1.		PINICC
2.	No Clues	DHOWREC
3.	Jumble Only	NTLEGSO
4.		KANSEL

How to play

Complete the crossword puzzle by looking at the clues and unscrambling the answers. When the puzzle is complete, unscramble the circled letters to solve the bonus.

CLUE: No Clues Jumble Only

BONUS ◯◯◯◯◯◯◯

JUMBLE® CROSSWORDS™

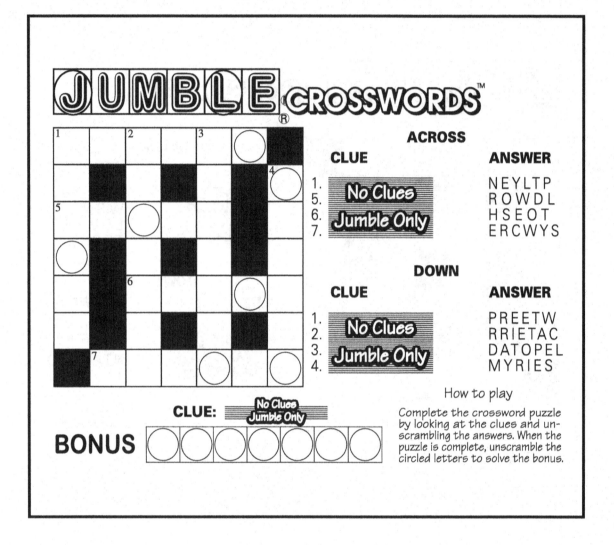

ACROSS

CLUE		ANSWER
1.	No Clues	N E Y L T P
5.		R O W D L
6.	Jumble Only	H S E O T
7.		E R C W Y S

DOWN

CLUE		ANSWER
1.	No Clues	P R E E T W
2.		R R I E T A C
3.	Jumble Only	D A T O P E L
4.		M Y R I E S

How to play

Complete the crossword puzzle by looking at the clues and un-scrambling the answers. When the puzzle is complete, unscramble the circled letters to solve the bonus.

CLUE: No Clues / Jumble Only

BONUS

ANSWERS

#1. Answers:
1A—BOSTON 5A—GIANT 6A—PARIS 7A—BOGOTÁ
1D—BIGWIG 2D—SHAMPOO 3D—ONTARIO 4D—RUSSIA
Bonus: ARUBA

#2 Answers:
1A—BANNER 5A—EXACT 6A—IDIOM 7A—EGRESS
1D—BLEACH 2D—NEARING 3D—ENTWINE 4D—COSMOS
Bonus: BOXING

#3 Answers:
1A—MOTIVE 5A—THEME 6A—FINDS 7A—THAMES
1D—MOTION 2D—TWELFTH 3D—VIETNAM 4D—ROASTS
Bonus: DETROIT

#4 Answers:
1A—ABACUS 5A—PRIZE 6A—THREW 7A—URCHIN
1D—APPEAL 2D—AVIATOR 3D—UNEARTH 4D—DARWIN
Bonus: NEW ZEALAND

#5 Answers:
1A—SHABBY 5A—RABID 6A—EDITS 7A—UTTERS
1D—STRONG 2D—AMBIENT 3D—BEDTIME 4D—FRISKS
Bonus: SIGNIFY

#6 Answers:
1A—MUSCLE 5A—SMELT 6A—TAINT 7A—ICEMAN
1D—MASCOT 2D—SKEPTIC 3D—LITHIUM 4D—BEATEN
Bonus: COLUMBIA

#7 Answers:
1A—UNWISE 5A—MOLAR 6A—OFTEN 7A—LETHAL
1D—UNMASK 2D—WELCOME 3D—SCRATCH 4D—SPINAL
Bonus: TAIWAN

#8 Answers:
1A—ALLURE 5A—GIVES 6A—BURST 7A—GENEVA
1D—ANGOLA 2D—LOVABLE 3D—RESERVE 4D—MARTHA
Bonus: BULGARIA

#9 Answers:
1A—POLICY 5A—SABLE 6A—RAISE 7A—LATENT
1D—PASTEL 2D—LIBERIA 3D—CREVICE 4D—MODEST
Bonus: MALAYSIA

#10 Answers:
1A—ENTITY 5A—PEPPY 6A—TROLL 7A—BRIDLE
1D—EXPECT 2D—TIPSTER 3D—THYROID 4D—TWELVE
Bonus: CRITTER

#11 Answers:
1A—UNKIND 5A—STYLE 6A—OILER 7A—CEASED
1D—UNSUNG 2D—KEYNOTE 3D—NEEDLES 4D—HORRID
Bonus: SHARKS

#12 Answers:
1A—GLOSSY 5A—EXTRA 6A—INGOT 7A—PEDDLE
1D—GREASE 2D—OUTLINE 3D—SNAGGED 4D—KETTLE
Bonus: KENNEDY

#13 Answers:
1A—NEARBY 5A—TAMPA 6A—ENACT 7A—ASHORE
1D—NITWIT 2D—AIMLESS 3D—BRAVADO 4D—LOATHE
Bonus: OPINION

#14 Answers:
1A—BICEPS 5A—BATON 6A—ALIEN 7A—USEFUL
1D—BOBCAT 2D—CUTLASS 3D—PONTIFF 4D—SIGNAL
Bonus: ATLANTIS

#15 Answers:
1A—MARVEL 5A—TIARA 6A—INLET 7A—FEEDER
1D—MUTUAL 2D—REALIZE 3D—ENABLED 4D—CASTER
Bonus: CEMENT

#16 Answers:
1A—TIGRIS 5A—STINT 6A—ANGER 7A—TERROR
1D—TESTED 2D—GRIMACE 3D—INTEGER 4D—POORER
Bonus: PATTON

#17 Answers:
1A—BEHOLD 5A—UPSET 6A—ICING 7A—TEAMED
1D—BRUISE 2D—HOSTILE 3D—LITHIUM 4D—FORGED
Bonus: CATFISH

#18 Answers:
1A—TAHITI 5A—TUDOR 6A—ORION 7A—ASCENT
1D—TUTORS 2D—HIDEOUS 3D—TURBINE 4D—MAGNET
Bonus: SUNSHINE

#19 Answers:
1A—IDIOMS 5A—PUPIL 6A—SNACK 7A—FEUDED
1D—IMPELS 2D—IMPASSE 3D—MALLARD 4D—BALKED
Bonus: COLUMBUS

#20 Answers:
1A—SHABBY 5A—CLING 6A—ORDER 7A—CANDID
1D—SICKLE 2D—ARIZONA 3D—BAGHDAD 4D—FEARED
Bonus: FAIRBANKS

#21 Answers:
1A—STURDY 5A—AMASS 6A—DREAM 7A—EDITOR
1D—STABLE 2D—UNAIDED 3D—DISSECT 4D—WARMER
Bonus: LAWYERS

#22 Answers:
1A—REVIVE 5A—LEMUR 6A—IDOLS 7A—BERETS
1D—RELIEF 2D—VAMPIRE 3D—VERBOSE 4D—NOISES
Bonus: BOB VILA

#23 Answers:
1A—APACHE 5A—HEFTY 6A—BRINK 7A—REVEAL
1D—ATHENS 2D—AFFABLE 3D—HAYWIRE 4D—NICKEL
Bonus: IN THE SEA

#24 Answers:
1A—BOGGLE 5A—DREAM 6A—ACORN 7A—TENNIS
1D—BEDLAM 2D—GRENADE 3D—LAMPOON 4D—DRINKS
Bonus: COOLIDGE

#25 Answers:
1A—TYRANT 5A—VISOR 6A—EVOKE 7A—STAKES
1D—TAVERN 2D—RESPECT 3D—NORFOLK 4D—STRESS
Bonus: POTATO

#26 Answers:
1A—UNKIND 5A—OTTER 6A—HOOCH 7A—SPOKEN
1D—UTOPIA 2D—KETCHUP 3D—NORFOLK 4D—URCHIN
Bonus: RUCKUS

#27 Answers:
1A—ECHOED 5A—LOSER 6A—ADAPT 7A—HECKLE
1D—ENLIST 2D—HOSTAGE 3D—EARMARK 4D—MANTLE
Bonus: CONTROL

#28 Answers:
1A—SUMMON 5A—RALLY 6A—RUPEE 7A—PARCEL
1D—SCREWY 2D—MALARIA 3D—OLYMPIC 4D—REVEAL
Bonus: ARMENIA

#29 Answers:
1A—CASTOR 5A—MERIT 6A—NOOSE 7A—SHREWD
1D—COMBAT 2D—SCRUNCH 3D—OUTCOME 4D—ASCEND
Bonus: STAR WARS

#30 Answers:
1A—NUMBER 5A—CREED 6A—TORCH 7A—LONDON
1D—NECTAR 2D—MAESTRO 3D—ENDURED 4D—NATHAN
Bonus: MADONNA

#31 Answers:
1A—RADISH 5A—APPLAUD 6A—TROOPER 7A—MENDED
1D—REALTY 2D—DEPLORE 3D—SWAMPED 4D—ADORED
Bonus: ODDITY

#32 Answers:
1A—COHORT 5A—FIRMS 6A—ELLIS 7A—STORES
1D—COFFER 2D—HARVEST 3D—RUSTLER 4D—AMUSES
Bonus: SITCOMS

#33 Answers:
1A—MOMENT 5A—BURST 6A—CROOK 7A—BEAKER
1D—MOBBED 2D—MIRACLE 3D—NETWORK 4D—TICKER
Bonus: TWOSOME

#34 Answers:
1A—MORTAL 5A—GRASS 6A—TONIC 7A—TRUCKS
1D—MIGHTY 2D—REALTOR 3D—ARSENIC 4D—SHOCKS
Bonus: HUMAN

#35 Answers:
1A—CLAUSE 5A—MAGMA 6A—REGAL 7A—LANDED
1D—CEMENT 2D—ALGERIA 3D—SNAGGED 4D—BAWLED
Bonus: BANANAS

#36 Answers:
1A—SOAKED 5A—GRASP 6A—SAUNA 7A—ADVENT
1D—SIGNAL 2D—AMASSED 3D—ESPOUSE 4D—INTACT
Bonus: CONVERSION

#37 Answers:
1A—UGANDA 5A—MOCHA 6A—INPUT 7A—MEANER
1D—UTMOST 2D—ASCRIBE 3D—DEADPAN 4D—OYSTER
Bonus: DYNAMITE

#38 Answers:
1A—UNEASY 5A—LOSER 6A—LYING 7A—UNVEIL
1D—UNLIKE 2D—EPSILON 3D—SURMISE 4D—BENGAL
Bonus: BOLIVIA

#39 Answers:
1A—PUBLIC 5A—NURSE 6A—AGAIN 7A—PANDAS
1D—PENCIL 2D—BARBARA 3D—IRELAND 4D—DRINKS
Bonus: BLANKS

#40 Answers:
1A—DAMAGE 5A—DINER 6A—RUGBY 7A—CHOSEN
1D—DODGED 2D—MONARCH 3D—GARAGES 4D—BUNYAN
Bonus: BERMUDA

#41 Answers:
1A—DOUBLE 5A—UPSET 6A—APRIL 7A—TELLER
1D—DEUCES 2D—UPSTAGE 3D—LITERAL 4D—HOLLER
Bonus: DECIPHER

#42 Answers:
1A—LUCENT 5A—STAIR 6A—IDOLS 7A—SMOKER
1D—LISBON 2D—CRANIUM 3D—NORFOLK 4D—GEYSER
Bonus: SIBLINGS

#43 Answers:
1A—DAMMED 5A—BADGE 6A—CLEAN 7A—SLATED
1D—DUBLIN 2D—MEDICAL 3D—ELEMENT 4D—RUINED
Bonus: SAMARITAN

#44 Answers:
1A—POTATO 5A—SHRUB 6A—IVORY 7A—FEUDED
1D—PISTOL 2D—TERMITE 3D—TABLOID 4D—BUOYED
Bonus: BOB HOPE

#45 Answers:
1A—MISHAP 5A—VIOLA 6A—KOALA 7A—PROTON
1D—MOVING 2D—SHOCKER 3D—ADAMANT 4D—RETAIN
Bonus: ETHIOPIA

#46 Answers:
1A—CACKLE 5A—PLUTO 6A—IRATE 7A—SLIDER
1D—COPPER 2D—CRUCIAL 3D—LEOPARD 4D—CAREER
Bonus: PAPER CLIP

#47 Answers:
1A—TWENTY 5A—ASPEN 6A—ACRES 7A—ANGLES
1D—THAMES 2D—EXPLAIN 3D—TENDRIL 4D—BURSTS
Bonus: BLUE WHALE

#48 Answers:
1A—NIMBLE 5A—VELUM 6A—RATED 7A—DAWDLE
1D—NOVICE 2D—MALARIA 3D—LIMITED 4D—TRUDGE
Bonus: VERDICT

#49 Answers:
1A—SWIPED 5A—AWFUL 6A—IMPEL 7A—STEERS
1D—SHABBY 2D—INFLICT 3D—ECLIPSE 4D—WORLDS
Bonus: SWORDFISH

#50 Answers:
1A—GADGET 5A—TINGE 6A—AGAIN 7A—SKATES
1D—GATHER 2D—DENMARK 3D—ELEGANT 4D—URANUS
Bonus: GANDHI

#51 Answers:
1A—PROMPT 5A—STYLE 6A—PLEAT 7A—SCOTCH
1D—PISCES 2D—OLYMPIC 3D—PRESENT 4D—SNATCH
Bonus: CLEOPATRA

#52 Answers:
1A—VERIFY 5A—COVER 6A—STAKE 7A—ADVERB
1D—VACUUM 2D—REVISED 3D—FORSAKE 4D—SUPERB
Bonus: MOBY DICK

#53 Answers:
1A—VACANT 5A—PLANT 6A—BLIMP 7A—TRAGIC
1D—VIPERS 2D—CLAMBER 3D—NOTHING 4D—TROPIC
Bonus: COLOMBIA

#54 Answers:
1A—EXPERT 5A—CHINA 6A—ACHES 7A—TENDON
1D—EXCUSE 2D—PRIMATE 3D—REACHED 4D—PERSON
Bonus: MIXED UP

#55 Answers:
1A—CRABBY 5A—ETHEL 6A—ENDOW 7A—MEAGER
1D—CLENCH 2D—ATHLETE 3D—BULLDOG 4D—ANSWER
Bonus: THE BAHAMAS

#56 Answers:
1A—SUNKEN 5A—LAURA 6A—RHINO 7A—CLIENT
1D—SILENT 2D—NEUTRAL 3D—EXAMINE 4D—EXTORT
Bonus: METEORITE

#57 Answers:
1A—UNSAID 5A—LURID 6A—TROOP 7A—CHISEL
1D—UNLESS 2D—STRETCH 3D—INDOORS 4D—CHAPEL
Bonus: HARRISON

#58 Answers:
1A—POWDER 5A—AMONG 6A—PIANO 7A—BRIDAL
1D—PLAGUE 2D—WHOPPER 3D—ENGLAND 4D—STROLL
Bonus: SUNDOWN

#59 Answers:
1A—JARGON 5A—ISSUE 6A—LADLE 7A—JEWELS
1D—JUICES 2D—RESOLVE 3D—OVERDUE 4D—BICEPS
Bonus: JAPANESE

#60 Answers:
1A—BATMAN 5A—SPELL 6A—THETA 7A—EDITED
1D—BASHED 2D—TREATED 3D—AILMENT 4D—POLAND
Bonus: SIBERIA

#61 Answers:
1A—INTACT 5A—AMISS 6A—ELUDE 7A—ATHENA
1D—ICARUS 2D—TRIDENT 3D—COSTUME 4D—AMOEBA
Bonus: ESCALATOR

#62 Answers:
1A—COWARD 5A—PLUTO 6A—DROIT 7A—EDISON
1D—COPPER 2D—WOUNDED 3D—RIOTOUS 4D—HASTEN
Bonus: THE LETTER O

#63 Answers:
1A—STABLE 5A—CLIMB 6A—TENSE 7A—PRUNED
1D—SOCKET 2D—AVIATOR 3D—LEBANON 4D—THREAD
Bonus: AUTOMOBILE

#64 Answers:
1A—TEMPER 5A—DONNA 6A—LYING 7A—ADONIS
1D—TEDIUM 2D—MANGLED 3D—ELATION 4D—BUDGES
Bonus: BADMINTON

#65 Answers:
1A—OTTAWA 5A—FEAST 6A—EXERT 7A—REASON
1D—OFFEND 2D—TRAPEZE 3D—WITNESS 4D—PHOTON
Bonus: HARRISON FORD

#66 Answers:
1A—BOGOTÁ 5A—FRANC 6A—PRIZE 7A—LESSON
1D—BUFFET 2D—GRAPPLE 3D—TACTICS 4D—SPLEEN
Bonus: RECOGNIZE

#67 Answers:
1A—BABBLE 5A—ACHES 6A—MEETS 7A—PASSED
1D—BEARER 2D—BOHEMIA 3D—LISTENS 4D—CURSED
Bonus: REPUBLICS

#68 Answers:
1A—EASILY 5A—CANON 6A—GOURD 7A—BLADES
1D—EXCITE 2D—SENEGAL 3D—LANGUID 4D—HORDES
Bonus: YOUR BREATH

#69 Answers:
1A—AMOUNT 5A—GAFFE 6A—COLIC 7A—TRADES
1D—ANGOLA 2D—OFFICER 3D—NEEDLED 4D—SLACKS
Bonus: LAST NAMES

#70 Answers:
1A—DUGOUT 5A—BOARD 6A—MEETS 7A—TRASHY
1D—DUBLIN 2D—GRAMMAR 3D—UNDRESS 4D—PIGSTY
Bonus: HUMAN BEING

#71 **Answers:**
1A—UTMOST 5A—PANDA 6A—LILAC 7A—ADORNS
1D—UMPIRE 2D—MINGLED 3D—STAPLER 4D—REACTS
Bonus: PROGRAM

#72 **Answers:**
1A—ACCESS 5A—SWAMP 6A—HOOPS 7A—ADHERE
1D—ABSORB 2D—CLASHED 3D—SUPPOSE 4D—LASSIE
Bonus: CAMBODIA

#73 **Answers:**
1A—DISMAY 5A—AVOID 6A—AMEND 7A—PHASES
1D—DRAGON 2D—STOMACH 3D—ADDRESS 4D—BLADES
Bonus: BAND—AID

#74 **Answers:**
1A—UNEVEN 5A—HAVOC 6A—LARVA 7A—SPOTTY
1D—UPHILL 2D—ENVELOP 3D—EXCERPT 4D—INFAMY
Bonus: SIX + FIVE = ELEVEN

#75 **Answers:**
1A—ENGINE 5A—CLUNG 6A—MERGE 7A—ATTAIN
1D—ESCAPE 2D—GOURMET 3D—NIGERIA 4D—MODERN
Bonus: DARLING

#76 **Answers:**
1A—BOGOTÁ 5A—HALVE 6A—LURID 7A—COMMIT
1D—BEHIND 2D—GALILEO 3D—THEOREM 4D—PUNDIT
Bonus: NOTHING

#77 **Answers:**
1A—TICKER 5A—CHIRP 6A—AMUCK 7A—MOMENT
1D—TICKLE 2D—CHICAGO 3D—ESPOUSE 4D—BUCKET
Bonus: MINUSCULE

#78 **Answers:**
1A—UNWRAP 5A—PERIL 6A—ALERT 7A—FESTER
1D—UMPIRE 2D—WARFARE 3D—AILMENT 4D—DOCTOR
Bonus: FLIPPED

#79 **Answers:**
1A—DOLLAR 5A—THING 6A—UNION 7A—LETHAL
1D—DETEST 2D—LEISURE 3D—ANGUISH 4D—SIGNAL
Bonus: STALLONE

#80 **Answers:**
1A—GODIVA 5A—BRAKE 6A—HUNCH 7A—JAMMED
1D—GOBLET 2D—DRACHMA 3D—VIETNAM 4D—MASHED
Bonus: ADJECTIVES

#81 **Answers:**
1A—SURFER 5A—TULIP 6A—EERIE 7A—BEIRUT
1D—SUTURE 2D—RELIEVE 3D—EMPEROR 4D—POTENT
Bonus: NILE RIVER

#82 **Answers:**
1A—HIATUS 5A—MIAMI 6A—SMIRK 7A—ODDEST
1D—HOMAGE 2D—AMASSED 3D—UNITIVE 4D—PACKET
Bonus: HARMONICA

#83 **Answers:**
1A—AGENCY 5A—FIFTH 6A—RABID 7A—KETTLE
1D—AFFAIR 2D—ENFORCE 3D—COHABIT 4D—PLEDGE
Bonus: PIGGY BANK

#84 **Answers:**
1A—RUMBLE 5A—BASRA 6A—ASSET 7A—AGENDA
1D—RABIES 2D—MUSTANG 3D—LIAISON 4D—MARTHA
Bonus: NUMBERED

#85 **Answers:**
1A—INVOKE 5A—TABBY 6A—ATTIC 7A—LEANED
1D—INTAKE 2D—VIBRATE 3D—KRYPTON 4D—PLACID
Bonus: BACKBONE

#86 **Answers:**
1A—FORMED 5A—BATHE 6A—AROMA 7A—STREAK
1D—FIBBED 2D—RETRACT 3D—EYESORE 4D—UNMASK
Bonus: AMADEUS

#87 **Answers:**
1A—BALKAN 5A—COTTA 6A—RISKY 7A—SLUDGE
1D—BECKON 2D—LITERAL 3D—AMASSED 4D—ENZYME
Bonus: NICK NOLTE

#88 **Answers:**
1A—DREARY 5A—FRILL 6A—EXERT 7A—OTTERS
1D—DEFACE 2D—EVIDENT 3D—RELIEVE 4D—GRATES
Bonus: DRAGONFLY

#89 **Answers:**
1A—SAMPLE 5A—CANON 6A—ALIEN 7A—BEAGLE
1D—SECURE 2D—MUNDANE 3D—LONGING 4D—ORANGE
Bonus: COLUMBO

#90 **Answers:**
1A—PEPPER 5A—MALTA 6A—CASED 7A—STODGY
1D—PUMMEL 2D—POLECAT 3D—ELAPSED 4D—FONDLY
Bonus: MARCO POLO

#91 **Answers:**
1A—SCHEME 5A—INDIA 6A—ACUTE 7A—ATTEST
1D—STIFLE 2D—HYDRANT 3D—MEASURE 4D—MOMENT
Bonus: SOUTH AFRICA

#92 **Answers:**
1A—TRAUMA 5A—ALIEN 6A—TEASE 7A—ERRANT
1D—TRAGIC 2D—AVIATOR 3D—MONTANA 4D—EFFECT
Bonus: LIFETIME

#93 **Answers:**
1A—UNWIND 5A—REALM 6A—HEIST 7A—GROGGY
1D—UNREST 2D—WEATHER 3D—NUMBING 4D—PASTRY
Bonus: TYPEWRITER

#94 **Answers:**
1A—AFFIRM 5A—PRONG 6A—RHINE 7A—ADVERB
1D—ASPECT 2D—FLOORED 3D—RAGTIME 4D—SUPERB
Bonus: AIR FORCE

#95 **Answers:**
1A—LOCATE 5A—GRUEL 6A—NAIVE 7A—EDISON
1D—LEGATO 2D—CHURNED 3D—TALLIES 4D—SCREEN
Bonus: ACREAGE

#96 **Answers:**
1A—WARSAW 5A—FEAST 6A—TIGHT 7A—ORNATE
1D—WAFFLE 2D—REALTOR 3D—ANTIGUA 4D—LOATHE
Bonus: EIGHT – FOUR = TWO + TWO

#97 **Answers:**
1A—PLUNGE 5A—WILDE 6A—ABATE 7A—PHRASE
1D—PEWTER 2D—UNLEASH 3D—GRENADA 4D—IMPEDE
Bonus: WARPED

#98 **Answers:**
1A—WEEVIL 5A—PLATO 6A—PEACE 7A—DEFEAT
1D—WIPERS 2D—EXAMPLE 3D—ISOLATE 4D—MOMENT
Bonus: NOVA SCOTIA

#99 **Answers:**
1A—COMICS 5A—LEMON 6A—NEARS 7A—JOLTED
1D—COLDLY 2D—MEMENTO 3D—CONTACT 4D—FUSSED
Bonus: JODIE FOSTER

#100 **Answers:**
1A—BUZZER 5A—SUAVE 6A—ACTOR 7A—ADORES
1D—BISHOP 2D—ZEALAND 3D—ERECTOR 4D—FERRIS
Bonus: CITIZENS

#101 **Answers:**
1A—SCORCH 5A—OCTET 6A—OSAKA 7A—SKIERS
1D—SMOOTH 2D—OUTLOOK 3D—COTTAGE 4D—CANALS
Bonus: SNICKERS

#102 **Answers:**
1A—AGENDA 5A—MOIST 6A—OTHER 7A—PEDDLE
1D—ARMADA 2D—EPISODE 3D—DITCHED 4D—HOARSE
Bonus: PROGRESS

#103 **Answers:**
1A—POTION 5A—THUMP 6A—DWELL 7A—CEASED
1D—PUTTER 2D—TRUNDLE 3D—OPPRESS 4D—KILLED
Bonus: TOM SELLECK

#104 **Answers:**
1A—TABLET 5A—ERROR 6A—AZTEC 7A—SNACKS
1D—THEORY 2D—BARGAIN 3D—ERRATIC 4D—WRECKS
Bonus: NOAH WEBSTER

#105 **Answers:**
1A—WINNER 5A—EXIST 6A—OZARK 7A—DIESEL
1D—WOEFUL 2D—NAIROBI 3D—ENTRAPS 4D—NICKEL
Bonus: ONE DOZEN

#106 **Answers:**
1A—LEGACY 5A—CRIER 6A—TEENS 7A—FROTHY
1D—LOCUST 2D—GLITTER 3D—CORRECT 4D—WHISKY
Bonus: TWENTY x FOUR = EIGHTY

#107 **Answers:**
1A—UNMASK 5A—FORLORN 6A—NOTES 7A—SCARED
1D—UNFAIR 2D—MORONIC 3D—SHOOTER 4D—UNUSED
Bonus: UNFAMILIAR

#108 **Answers:**
1A—SCHEME 5A—MACON 6A—SCARF 7A—SWEETS
1D—SIMPLE 2D—HACKSAW 3D—MUNDANE 4D—STUFFS
Bonus: WAFFLE IRON

#109 **Answers:**
1A—COVERT 5A—TONGS 6A—UNITE 7A—DETECT
1D—CITRUS 2D—VENTURE 3D—RESPITE 4D—ABSENT
Bonus: COVENANT

#110 **Answers:**
1A—JAGUAR 5A—SLITS 6A—MERIT 7A—DREARY
1D—JOSTLE 2D—GLIMMER 3D—AUSTRIA 4D—FILTHY
Bonus: TAJ MAHAL

#111 **Answers:**
1A—MORSEL 5A—HOARD 6A—TEENS 7A—TRUSTY
1D—MOHAWK 2D—REACTOR 3D—ENDLESS 4D—CRUSTY
Bonus: HUMAN EYE

#112 **Answers:**
1A—ATTAIN 5A—GUSTO 6A—IRONS 7A—EGRESS
1D—AUGUST 2D—TASTING 3D—ISOTOPE 4D—VERSES
Bonus: SEA OTTER

#113 **Answers:**
1A—PLENTY 5A—CHILI 6A—UNTIL 7A—READER
1D—PACKED 2D—EPICURE 3D—TAINTED 4D—TELLER
Bonus: PLANET EARTH

#114 **Answers:**
1A—PADDED 5A—ISSUE 6A—OMEGA 7A—HECTIC
1D—PLIANT 2D—DISROBE 3D—ELEMENT 4D—MOSAIC
Bonus: HUMAN MIND

#115 **Answers:**
1A—SPRITE 5A—GECKO 6A—UPPER 7A—BEARER
1D—SIGNAL 2D—RECLUSE 3D—TROOPER 4D—NEARER
Bonus: BALLPOINT PEN

#116 **Answers:**
1A—EUROPE 5A—STORM 6A—INKED 7A—ORANGE
1D—ENSUES 2D—ROOMIER 3D—PUMPKIN 4D—CANDLE
Bonus: KNEECAPS

#117 **Answers:**
1A—SPLICE 5A—MONET 6A—EVADE 7A—UNISON
1D—SYMBOL 2D—LANTERN 3D—CUTLASS 4D—CAVERN
Bonus: COLOR—BLIND

#118 **Answers:**
1A—ENGINE 5A—STOIC 6A—POSSE 7A—EDWARD
1D—ENSUED 2D—GROUPED 3D—NICOSIA 4D—INDEED
Bonus: SINGAPORE

#119 **Answers:**
1A—TICKET 5A—COINS 6A—INEPT 7A—BEINGS
1D—TICKER 2D—CUISINE 3D—EASTERN 4D—MONTHS
Bonus: PARKING METER

#120 **Answers:**
1A—SUPPLY 5A—DENIM 6A—IRISH 7A—LEAGUE
1D—SEDATE 2D—PENSIVE 3D—LEMMING 4D—ARCHIE
Bonus: CASPIAN SEA

#121 **Answers:**
1A—REDUCE 5A—NEPAL 6A—OLIVE 7A—JARGON
1D—RINSED 2D—DIPLOMA 3D—CALLING 4D—GOVERN
Bonus: INDIANA JONES

#122 **Answers:**
1A—GARAGE 5A—IGLOO 6A—INPUT 7A—CHERRY
1D—GUITAR 2D—RALEIGH 3D—GROUPER 4D—CHATTY
Bonus: TONY THE TIGER

#123 **Answers:**
1A—PORTAL 5A—COWER 6A—IDAHO 7A—SEVERS
1D—PACKED 2D—REWRITE 3D—ACREAGE 4D—SCOOTS
Bonus: WOODPECKERS

#124 **Answers:**
1A—GROOVE 5A—BATCH 6A—OCCUR 7A—HEREBY
1D—GOBLIN 2D—OUTCOME 3D—VEHICLE 4D—STORMY
Bonus: BLUEBERRIES

#125 **Answers:**
1A—STAPLE 5A—AARON 6A—NAIVE 7A—MERGED
1D—SCARED 2D—ARRANGE 3D—LONGING 4D—LEGEND
Bonus: CAMP DAVID

#126 **Answers:**
1A—HOGWASH 5A—RULER 6A—LINDA 7A—SLOWEST
1D—HARNESS 2D—GALILEO 3D—ARRANGE
4D—HYDRANT
Bonus: STONEHENGE

#127 **Answers:**
1A—ARMADA 5A—FACET 6A—ATOLL 7A—PLATES
1D—AFFAIR 2D—MICHAEL 3D—DETROIT 4D—BUGLES
Bonus: ALPHABETICAL

#128 **Answers:**
1A—PERUSE 5A—EXTRA 6A—NEPAL 7A—CANDID
1D—PLEDGE 2D—ROTUNDA 3D—SWAMPED 4D—POLLED
Bonus: DOLLAR SIGN

#129 **Answers:**
1A—NABBED 5A—BLEEP 6A—IVORY 7A—MELTED
1D—NOBODY 2D—BEEHIVE 3D—EXPLOIT 4D—PLAYED
Bonus: ONE DOLLAR BILL

#130 **Answers:**
1A—PALTRY 5A—DAWNS 6A—RHINE 7A—SWEDEN
1D—PUDDLE 2D—LOWBROW 3D—RESCIND 4D—PIGEON
Bonus: DISNEY WORLD

#131 **Answers:**
1A—LEGION 5A—BRAWL 6A—DIGIT 7A—PANDAS
1D—LABELS 2D—GRANDMA 3D—OBLIGED 4D—CHUTES
Bonus: GIRL SCOUTS

#132 **Answers:**
1A—ATTUNE 5A—FEAST 6A—HABIT 7A—GAVELS
1D—AFFECT 2D—TRACHEA 3D—NOTABLE 4D—DEATHS
Bonus: FIDGET **Bonus:** GIFTED

#133 **Answers:**
1A—IODINE 5A—FIRST 6A—BEING 7A—MERGES
1D—INFUSE 2D—DURABLE 3D—NOTHING 4D—STAGES
Bonus: GRUDGE **Bonus:** RUGGED

#134 **Answers:**
1A—TENDER 5A—STUNG 6A—REACT 7A—SLIDES
1D—TESTED 2D—NEUTRAL 3D—ENGLAND 4D—GRATIS
Bonus: GADGET **Bonus:** TAGGED

#135 **Answers:**
1A—GANDHI 5A—MUTES 6A—RAISE 7A—ALBEIT
1D—GAMBIT 2D—NATURAL 3D—HOSTILE 4D—INFEST
Bonus: FINISHED **Bonus:** FIENDISH

#136 **Answers:**
1A—BUMPER 5A—VERDI 6A—NIECE 7A—SCOTCH
1D—BOVINE 2D—MORONIC 3D—EVIDENT 4D—JOSEPH
Bonus: BEDROOM **Bonus:** BOREDOM

#137 **Answers:**
1A—GOSPEL 5A—BLURB 6A—FIEND 7A—CENSUS
1D—GIBBON 2D—SHUFFLE 3D—EMBLEMS 4D—GUIDES
Bonus: REGGIE **Bonus:** GEIGER

#138 **Answers:**
1A—AUTUMN 5A—SUDAN 6A—LILAC 7A—BRIDGE
1D—ASSERT 2D—TODDLER 3D—MINGLED 4D—CIRCLE
Bonus: ADMIRER **Bonus:** MARRIED

#139 **Answers:**
1A—PAMPER 5A—RALPH 6A—IMBUE 7A—SECTOR
1D—PARSEC 2D—MALAISE 3D—EXHIBIT 4D—ENDEAR
Bonus: MENTORS **Bonus:** MONSTER

#140 **Answers:**
1A—INHALE 5A—RIPEN 6A—EVADE 7A—ASPENS
1D—ISRAEL 2D—HAPLESS 3D—LINKAGE 4D—DURESS
Bonus: REVERSED **Bonus:** RESERVED

#141 **Answers:**
1A—GROUND 5A—PETER 6A—ROUGH 7A—COVERT
1D—GOPHER 2D—ONTARIO 3D—NURTURE 4D—UPSHOT
Bonus: PATCHING **Bonus:** NIGHTCAP

#142 **Answers:**
1A—THWART 5A—AMONG 6A—POISE 7A—GREECE
1D—TRACED 2D—WHOPPER 3D—RAGTIME 4D—IMPEDE
Bonus: APHRODITE **Bonus:** ATROPHIED

#143 **Answers:**
1A—REPORT 5A—FLOSS 6A—LYING 7A—FRIDAY
1D—REFUND 2D—PROWLER 3D—RESCIND 4D—SHAGGY
Bonus: POISONED **Bonus:** POSEIDON

#144 **Answers:**
1A—REDUCE 5A—DEPOT 6A—EVADE 7A—LESSON
1D—RADISH 2D—DEPLETE 3D—CUTLASS 4D—GOVERN
Bonus: CREDITOR **Bonus:** DIRECTOR

#145 **Answers:**
1A—ADVISE 5A—PASTA 6A—BOGUS 7A—HEYDAY
1D—ASPECT 2D—VISIBLE 3D—SNAGGED 4D—TRUSTY
Bonus: DIAPERS **Bonus:** PRAISED **Bonus:** DESPAIR

#146 **Answers:**
1A—SHRINK 5A—AMONG 6A—TOTEM 7A—GRUDGE
1D—SEALED 2D—ROOSTER 3D—NEGATED 4D—STYMIE
Bonus: MARKER **Bonus:** REMARK **Bonus:** KRAMER

#147 **Answers:**
1A—DINNER 5A—EDITH 6A—ORBIT 7A—PISTIL
1D—DREARY 2D—NAIROBI 3D—EXHIBIT 4D—CARTEL
Bonus: DANIEL **Bonus:** DENIAL **Bonus:** NAILED

#148 **Answers:**
1A—POTION 5A—BACON 6A—FABLE 7A—CLOSED
1D—PUBLIC 2D—TACTFUL 3D—OMNIBUS 4D—INDEED
Bonus: TOPSIDE **Bonus:** DEPOSIT **Bonus:** POSITED

#149 **Answers:**
1A—LATEST 5A—BLUFF 6A—POINT 7A—STRESS
1D—LOBBED 2D—TRUMPET 3D—SUFFICE 4D—GRATES
Bonus: DUELING **Bonus:** ELUDING **Bonus:** INDULGE

#150 **Answers:**
1A—ANGOLA 5A—BASIS 6A—UNION 7A—WEIGHT
1D—ALBUMS 2D—GESTURE 3D—LASTING 4D—MAGNET
Bonus: MARTIAN **Bonus:** MARTINA **Bonus:** TAMARIN

#151 **Answers:**
1A—DOCILE 5A—PLUMB 6A—LARGO 7A—ASSAIL
1D—DEPEND 2D—COUPLES 3D—LIBERIA 4D—STROLL
Bonus: AUCTIONED **Bonus:** CAUTIONED
Bonus: EDUCATION

#152 **Answers:**
1A—ENIGMA 5A—OFTEN 6A—GUISE 7A—FRANCE
1D—EVOLVE 2D—INTEGER 3D—MENTION 4D—SLEEVE
Bonus: LETTERS **Bonus:** SETTLER **Bonus:** TRESTLE

#153 **Answers:**
1A—STEADY 5A—PIPES 6A—RAISE 7A—ORIGIN
1D—SUPPLY 2D—EMPEROR 3D—DASHING 4D—CAVERN
Bonus: CLAIMED **Bonus:** DECIMAL **Bonus:** MEDICAL

#154 **Answers:**
1A—SEWING 5A—CRIMP 6A—POUND 7A—ARTERY
1D—SECTOR 2D—WHISPER 3D—NEPTUNE 4D—AVIDLY
Bonus 1: PITCHER **Bonus 2:** POSITION

#155 **Answers:**
1A—SHABBY 5A—EXTRA 6A—MAKER 7A—STITCH
1D—SCENIC 2D—ATTEMPT 3D—BLANKET 4D—SCORCH
Bonus 1: SCIENCE **Bonus 2:** CHEMISTRY

#156 **Answers:**
1A—SCRIPT 5A—PLUTO 6A—DEUCE 7A—ADHERE
1D—SEPTIC 2D—ROUNDED 3D—PROCURE 4D—SNEEZE
Bonus 1: ELECTION **Bonus 2:** PRESIDENT

#157 **Answers:**
1A—SHOVED 5A—PLUMB 6A—ERASE 7A—STREET
1D—SOPHIA 2D—OPULENT 3D—EMBRACE 4D—COVERT
Bonus 1: COMPOSER **Bonus 2:** BEETHOVEN

#158 **Answers:**
1A—ENGULF 5A—COMET 6A—AHEAD 7A—STAYED
1D—EXCITE 2D—GYMNAST 3D—LOTTERY 4D—WINDED
Bonus 1: OUTFIT **Bonus 2:** CLOTHING

#159 **Answers:**
1A—SWITCH 5A—GIVES 6A—LAIRS 7A—PENNED
1D—SUGARY 2D—INVOLVE 3D—CUSHION 4D—MISSED
Bonus 1: TV SHOWS **Bonus 2:** PROGRAMS

#160 **Answers:**
1A—WAIVED 5A—REVUE 6A—LEGAL 7A—EDISON
1D—WARMTH 2D—INVALID 3D—EMERGES 4D—STALIN
Bonus 1: VILLIAN **Bonus 2:** DARTH VADER

#161 **Answers:**
1A—JINGLE 5A—BARON 6A—ALICE 7A—TARGET
1D—JABBED 2D—NIRVANA 3D—LANDING 4D—HONEST
Bonus 1: BRIGHT **Bonus 2:** ADJECTIVE

#162 **Answers:**
1A—THEORY 5A—FALLS 6A—PAINT 7A—DELETE
1D—TOFFEE 2D—ECLIPSE 3D—RESPITE 4D—HURTLE
Bonus 1: CLOUDY **Bonus 2:** RAINFALL

#163 **Answers:**
1A—VERMIN 5A—NOTES 6A—LLAMA 7A—ARCTIC
1D—VANDAL 2D—RATTLER 3D—INSTANT 4D—MOSAIC
Bonus 1: ISLAND **Bonus 2:** TASMANIA

#164 **Answers:**
1A—GANDHI 5A—LEARN 6A—ELBOW 7A—STAGES
1D—GALORE 2D—NEAREST 3D—HANDBAG 4D—FROWNS
Bonus 1: GOLFER **Bonus 2:** BEN HOGAN

#165 **Answers:**
1A—BASALT 5A—AROMA 6A—SULKS 7A—PROTON
1D—BEAGLE 2D—SPONSOR 3D—LEAFLET 4D—HUDSON
Bonus 1: EUROPE **Bonus 2:** PORTUGAL

#166 **Answers:**
1A—LEGION 5A—ROOST 6A—LIMBO 7A—ADONIS
1D—LARYNX 2D—GROWLED 3D—OTTOMAN 4D—SHOOTS
Bonus 1: OREGON **Bonus 2:** NORTHWEST

#167 **Answers:**
1A—GUITAR 5A—SKIMP 6A—AWARE 7A—VENDOR
1D—GOSSIP 2D—IMITATE 3D—APPLAUD 4D—CAREER
Bonus: ENIGMA

#168 **Answers:**
1A—PICKLE 5A—ADOPT 6A—DARTS 7A—GRILLS
1D—PEANUT 2D—CHOWDER 3D—LITERAL 4D—NOISES
Bonus: UNCERTAIN

#169 **Answers:**
1A—MILDEW 5A—FATAL 6A—UPPER 7A—RECESS
1D—MUFFLE 2D—LETTUCE 3D—ECLIPSE 4D—SHARKS
Bonus: CLUELESS

#170 **Answers:**
1A—VACUUM 5A—AZTEC 6A—COVET 7A—DEGREE
1D—VIABLE 2D—CUTICLE 3D—UNCOVER 4D—SETTLE
Bonus: OBSCURE

#171 **Answers:**
1A—AZALEA 5A—PIANO 6A—EXILE 7A—FRENZY
1D—ASPECT 2D—AMATEUR 3D—EROSION 4D—GREEDY
Bonus: PUZZLING

#172 **Answers:**
1A—BUFFET 5A—MERGE 6A—HYENA 7A—PRETTY
1D—BUMPED 2D—FURTHER 3D—EVEREST 4D—UNEASY
Bonus: STUMPED

#173 **Answers:**
1A—UNSURE 5A—FROWN 6A—ALIKE 7A—SHAGGY
1D—UNFAIR 2D—STOMACH 3D—RUNNING 4D—COMEDY
Bonus: SOLUTION

#174 **Answers:**
1A—BAMBOO 5A—TENET 6A—THEIR 7A—GRILLS
1D—BOTTOM 2D—MONITOR 3D—OATMEAL 4D—SPORTS
Bonus: PROBLEM

#175 **Answers:**
1A—MUSCLE 5A—EXACT 6A—PRUNE 7A—POTENT
1D—MEEKLY 2D—SHAMPOO 3D—LETTUCE 4D—ORIENT
Bonus: PERPLEX

#176 **Answers:**
1A—PICKLE 5A—CROWN 6A—DWELL 7A—BRUTUS
1D—PICNIC 2D—CHOWDER 3D—LONGEST 4D—ANKLES
Bonus: UNKNOWN

#177 **Answers:**
1A—PLENTY 5A—WORLD 6A—THOSE 7A—SCREWY
1D—PEWTER 2D—ERRATIC 3D—TADPOLE 4D—MISERY
Bonus: MYSTERY

Need More Jumbles®?

Jumble® Books

More than 175 puzzles each!

Animal Jumble®
$9.95 • ISBN 1-57243-197-0

Jumble® at Work
$9.95 • ISBN 1-57243-147-4

Jumble® Fun
$9.95 • ISBN 1-57243-379-5

Jumble® Grab Bag
$9.95 • ISBN 1-57243-273-X

Jumble® Jubilee
$9.95 • ISBN 1-57243-231-4

Jumble® Junction
$9.95 • ISBN 1-57243-380-9

Jumble® Madness
$9.95 • ISBN 1-892049-24-4

Jumble® See & Search
$9.95 • ISBN 1-57243-549-6

Jumble® Surprise
$9.95 • ISBN 1-57243-320-5

Romance Jumble®
$9.95 • ISBN 1-57243-146-6

Sports Jumble®
$9.95 • ISBN 1-57243-113-X

Summer Fun Jumble®
$9.95 • ISBN 1-57243-114-8

Travel Jumble®
$9.95 • ISBN 1-57243-198-9

TV Jumble®
$9.95 • ISBN 1-57243-462-7

Jumble® Fever
$9.95 • ISBN 1-57243-593-3

Hollywood Jumble® BrainBusters™

Hollywood Jumble® BrainBusters™
$9.95 • ISBN: 1-57243-594-1

More than 175 puzzles!

Oversize Jumble® Books

Generous Jumble®
$19.95 • ISBN 1-57243-385-X

Giant Jumble®
$19.95 • ISBN 1-57243-349-3

Gigantic Jumble®
$19.95 • ISBN 1-57243-426-0

Jumbo Jumble®
$19.95 • ISBN 1-57243-314-0

Colossal Jumble®
$19.95 • ISBN 1-57243-490-2

More than 500 puzzles each!

Jumble® Crosswords™

Jumble® Crosswords™
$9.95 • ISBN 1-57243-347-7

More Jumble® Crosswords™
$9.95 • ISBN 1-57243-386-8

Jumble® Crosswords™ Adventure
$9.95 • ISBN 1-57243-462-7

Jumble® Crosswords™ Challenge
$9.95 • ISBN 1-57243-423-6

More than 175 puzzles each!

Jumble® BrainBusters

Jumble® BrainBusters
$9.95 • ISBN: 1-892049-28-7

Jumble® BrainBusters II
$9.95 • ISBN: 1-57243-424-4

Jumble® BrainBusters III
$9.95 • ISBN: 1-57243-463-5

Jumble® BrainBusters IV
$9.95 • ISBN: 1-57243-489-9

Jumble® BrainBusters 5
$9.95 • ISBN: 1-57243-548-8

More than 175 puzzles each!

Jumble® BrainBusters Junior

Jumble® BrainBusters Junior
$9.95 • ISBN: 1-892049-29-5

Jumble® BrainBusters Junior II
$9.95 • ISBN: 1-57243-425-2

More than 175 puzzles each!